GOD IS CLOSER
THAN YOU THINK

Resources by John Ortberg

Everybody's Normal Till You Get to Know Them
(book, ebook, audio)

God Is Closer Than You Think
(book, ebook, audio, curriculum with Stephen and Amanda Sorenson)

*If You Want to Walk on Water,
You've Got to Get Out of the Boat*
(book, ebook, audio, curriculum with Stephen and Amanda Sorenson)

Know Doubt
(book, ebook, previously titled Faith and Doubt)

The Life You've Always Wanted
(book, ebook, audio, curriculum with Stephen and Amanda Sorenson)

Love Beyond Reason

The Me I Want to Be
(book, ebook, audio, curriculum with Scott Rubin)

Soul Keeping
(book, ebook, curriculum with Christine M. Anderson)

When the Game Is Over, It All Goes Back in the Box
(book, ebook, audio, curriculum with Stephen and Amanda Sorenson)

Who Is This Man?
(book, ebook, audio, curriculum with Christine M. Anderson)

JOHN ORTBERG

GOD IS CLOSER

THAN YOU THINK

ZONDERVAN®
.com

WILLOW
Willow Creek Resources

ZONDERVAN

God Is Closer Than You Think
Copyright © 2005 by John Ortberg

This title is also available as a Zondervan ebook product.
Visit www.zondervan.com/ebooks for more information.

This title is also available as a Zondervan audio product.
Visit www.zondervan.com/audiopages for more information.

Requests for information should be addressed to:

Zondervan, 3900 Sparks Dr. SE, Grand Rapids, Michigan 49546

This edition: ISBN 978-0-310-34047-8 (softcover)

Library of Congress Cataloging-in-Publication Data

Ortberg, John.
    God is closer than you think / John Ortberg. — 1st ed.
       p. cm.
    Includes bibliographical references and index.
    ISBN 978-0-310-25349-5 (hardcover)
    1. Presence of God.   2. Christian life — Presbyterian authors.   I. Title.
BV4509.5.O78 2005
248.4 — dc22

                                2004024716

Some names and details have been changed in order to protect the privacy of people involved in true stories told in this book.

The Scripture versions used in this book are listed on page 169, which hereby becomes a part of this copyright page. Italics in quotations of Scripture have been added by the author for emphasis.

Any Internet addresses (websites, blogs, etc.) and telephone numbers in this book are offered as a resource. They are not intended in any way to be or imply an endorsement by Zondervan, nor does Zondervan vouch for the content of these sites and numbers for the life of this book.

Interior design by Michelle Espinoza

Printed in the United States of America

14 15 16 17 18 19 /QG/ 20 19 18 17 16 15 14 13 12 11 10 9 8 7 6 5 4 3 2 1

To Laura, Mallory, and Johnny;
for Winston and Milo and Spotty and Jo-Jo;
for the furnace man and Ralph the Tree and Fred the Bread;
for the barn story and Bugs Meany and Norman Bates
and Portillo's and all the times I saved the president's life;
for the gift that binds my anniversary and
Thanksgiving and Groundhog Day;
for doughnut runs and dollar days
and thin places in the hedge ...

And to Nancy

CONTENTS

ACKNOWLEDGMENTS

In the course of writing this book I moved from the Midwest to California and joined the staff of Menlo Park Presbyterian Church. I am very grateful to the people of MPPC for giving me time to write and offering such a loving community to be a part of. John Mumford provided a place to write that gave me a look at what novelist Wallace Stegner called "the last sunset on the continent"; any lack of inspiration is due to me and not the view. Trudi Barnes partnered with extraordinary energy to make this project and so much other ministry possible.

Peets Coffee kept what neurons I have in firing mode.

This marks the fifth book I have written with Zondervan, and I am grateful for the sense of partnership that has deepened with each one. Jack Kuhatschek offered countless hours of conversation and thought. John Topliff and Greg Stielstra combine wisdom and soulishness with savvy and energy. Jim Ruark polished the prose. Scott Bolinder and Stan Gundry and the rest of the team have made it a kind of writing home for which I am deeply grateful.

Both Liz Heaney and Evelyn Bence offered many helpful suggestions.

As always, the thought and work of Dallas Willard was never far away when I was writing.

But my favorite collaborator on this project was Mallory Ortberg. She edited the entire manuscript in an early draft, made too many contributions to count, and wrote material that took my breath away. Someday, if I'm lucky, she may let me edit some of her stuff.

GOD'S GREAT DESIRE

For over the margins of life comes a whisper, a faint call, a premonition of richer living....

Thomas Kelly

During the first year of our marriage, Nancy and I spent two months traveling around Europe. We lived on a budget of $13.50 per day for food, lodging, and entertainment. We breakfasted every morning on bread and cheese. We lodged in accommodations compared with which the Bates Motel in the movie *Psycho* would be an upgrade. Entertainment on that budget consisted of buying *Time* magazine once a week and ripping it in half so we could both read it at the same time.

We splurged in Italy, where we blew one whole day's allowance on a single meal and spent money we could not afford to look at the treasures of Western art. The highlight of the day came after standing in line for hours at the Vatican to view Michelangelo Buonarroti's brilliant painting of God and Adam on the ceiling of the Sistine Chapel. His masterpiece is one of two works of art that serve as touchstones for this book. (I'm saving the other one for the next chapter.) If you look carefully at the painting, you notice that the figure of God is extended toward the man with great vigor. He twists his body to move it as close to the man as possible. His head is turned toward the man, and his gaze is fixed on him. God's arm is stretched out, his index finger extended straight forward; every muscle is taut.

Before Michelangelo, art scholars say, the standard paintings of creation showed God standing on the ground, in effect helping Adam to his feet. Not here. This God is rushing toward Adam on a cloud, one of the "chariots of heaven," propelled by the angels. (In our day they don't look quite aerobicized enough to move really fast, but in Michelangelo's day the angels suggested power and swiftness.) It is as if even in the midst of the splendor of all creation, God's entire being is wrapped up in his impatient desire to close the gap between himself and this man. He can't wait. His hand comes within a hairbreadth of the man's hand.

The painting is traditionally called *The Creation of Adam,* but some scholars say it should be called *The Endowment of Adam.* Adam has already been given physical life—his eyes are open, and he is conscious. What is happening is that he is being offered life *with* God. "All of man's potential, physical and spiritual, is contained in this one timeless moment," writes one art critic.

Apparently one of the messages that Michelangelo wanted to convey is God's implacable determination to reach out to and be with the person he has created. God is as close as he can be. But having come that close, he allows just a little space, so that Adam can choose. He waits for Adam to make his move.

Adam is more difficult to interpret. His arm is partially extended toward God, but his body reclines in a lazy pose, leaning backward as if he has no interest at all in making a connection. Maybe he assumes that God, having come this far, will close the gap. Maybe he is indifferent to the possibility of touching his creator. Maybe he lacks the strength. All he would have to do is lift a finger.

The fresco took Michelangelo four years of intense labor. The physical demands of standing on a scaffold painting above his head were torture. (*"I have my beard turned to the ceiling, my head bent back on my shoulders, my chest arched like that of a Harpy; my brush drips on to my face and makes me look like a decorated pavement.... I am bent taut like a Syrian bow."*) Because he was forced to look upwards for hours while painting, he eventually could only read a letter if he held it at arm's length above his head. One night, exhausted by his work, alone with his doubts, discouraged by a project that was too great for him, he wrote in his journal a single sentence: "I am no painter."

Yet for nearly half a millennium this picture has spoken of God's great desire to be with the human beings he has made in his own image. Perhaps Michelangelo was not alone in his work after all. Perhaps the God who was so near to Adam was near to Michelangelo as well—at work in his mind and his eye and his brushes.

THE "EVERYWHERENESS" OF GOD

This picture reminds us: God is closer than we think. He is never farther than a prayer away. All it takes is the barest effort, the lift of a finger. Every moment—this moment right now, as you read these words—is the "one timeless moment" of divine endowment, of life with God.

"This is my Father's world," an old song says. "He shines in all that's fair.... In the rustling grass I hear him pass, he speaks to me everywhere." The Scriptures are full of what might be called the *everywhereness* of God's speaking. "The heavens are telling the glory of God; ... day to day pours forth speech."

He talks through burning bushes and braying donkeys; he sends messages through storms and rainbows and earthquakes and dreams, he whispers in a still small voice. He speaks (in the words of Garrison Keillor) in "ordinary things like cooking and small talk, through storytelling, making love, fishing, tending animals and sweet corn and flowers, through sports, music, and books, raising kids—all the places where the gravy soaks in and grace shines through."

GOD'S GREAT DESIRE

The story of the Bible isn't primarily about the desire of people to be with God; it's the desire of God to be with people.

One day I was sitting on a plane next to a businessman. The screen saver on his computer was the picture of a towheaded little boy taking what looked like his first shaky step. "Is that your son?" I asked. Big mistake.

Yes, that was the man's son, his only child. Let's say his name was Adam. The picture on the computer was taken three months earlier, when Adam was eleven months old. The man told me about his son's first step and first word with a sense of wonder, as if Adam had invented locomotion and speech. There was a more recent picture of Adam on the man's palm pilot. The man showed it to me. The same picture could be viewed more clearly on the computer. The man showed me that. He had a whole string of pictures of Adam doing things that pretty much all children do, and he displayed them one at a time. With commentary. I and my seatmates got a graduate course in Adamology.

"I can't wait to get home to him," the man said. "In the meantime, I could look at these pictures a hundred times a day. They never get old to me." (They were already getting pretty tiresome to everybody else in our section of the plane.)

Why was the man so preoccupied with Adam? Was it because the boy's achievements were so impressive? No. Millions of children learn to do the same thing every day. My own children (I wanted to tell him) had done the same things at an earlier age with superior skill.

The man was preoccupied with Adam because he looked at him through the eyes of a father. Everything Adam did was cloaked with wonder. It didn't matter that other children do them as well.

"You obviously miss your son," I said. "How long ago did you leave home?"

Yesterday.

One day away from his son is one too many. So he was rushing through the skies, taking a chariot through the clouds, implacably determined to be at home with his child. He didn't simply want to love his son from a distance. He wanted to *be with him.*

And then it hit me. I am the child on God's screen saver. And so are you. The tiniest details of our lives never grow old to him. God himself is filled with wonder at our faltering steps and stammering words—not because we do them better than anyone else, but because he views them through the eyes of a loving Father. God shows our pictures to the angels until even the angels get a little tired of looking. And the story of the Bible is first of all God's story—the story of a father rushing through the clouds to be at home with you. One day apart is one day too many.

THE PRIMARY PROMISE: I WILL BE *WITH* YOU

The central promise in the Bible is not "I will forgive you," although of course that promise is there. It is not the promise of life after death, although we are offered that as well. The most frequent promise in the Bible is "I will be *with* you."

Before Adam and Eve ever sinned or needed forgiveness, they were promised God's presence. He would walk with them in the cool of the day.

The promise came to Enoch, who "walked with God." It was made to Noah, to Abraham and Sarah, to Jacob and Joseph and Moses and David and Amos and Mary and Paul and too many others to list. It is the reason for courage: "Do not be terrified;... for the LORD your God will be *with you* wherever you go." It kept them going in darkness: "Yea, though I walk through the valley of the shadow of death, I will fear no evil: for thou art *with me.*"

God gave Israel the tabernacle and the ark of the covenant and manna and the temple and a pillar of cloud and another one of fire, like so many Post-It notes saying, "Don't forget. I am *with you.*"

When God himself came to earth, his redemptive name was *Immanuel*—God *with us.* When Jesus left, his promise was to send the Spirit so that "I am *with you* always, even to the end of the age."

At the end of time, when sin is a distant and defeated memory and forgiveness is as obsolete as buggy whips, it will be sung, "God's dwelling place is now among the people, and he will dwell with them. They will be his people, and God himself will be with them and be their God."

The central promise in the Bible is not "I will forgive you." The most frequent promise is "I will be with *you."*

"The unity of the Bible is discovered in the development of life-with-God as a reality on earth, centered in the person of Jesus," write

Dallas Willard and Richard Foster. God is determined that you should be in every respect his friend, his companion, his dwelling place.

"I CAN FEEL HIM WALKING AROUND ..."

"Find a place in your heart," said an ancient sage named Theophan the Recluse, "and speak there with the Lord. It is the Lord's reception room." Some people seem to find this room easily. Friends of ours have a daughter who said when she was five years old, "I know Jesus lives in my heart, because when I put my hand on it I can feel him walking around in there."

Sofia Cavalletti is a researcher who has pioneered the study of spirituality in young children. She finds that children often have an amazing perception that far surpasses what they've already been taught. One three-year-old girl, raised in an atheistic family with no church contact and no Bible in the home, asked her father, "Where did the world come from?" He answered her in strictly naturalistic, scientific terms. Then he added, "There are some people who say that all this comes from a very powerful being, and they call him God."

At this, the little girl started dancing around the room with joy: "I knew what you told me wasn't true—it's him, it's him!"

Writer Anne Lamott was raised by her dad to be a devout atheist. She and her siblings all had to agree to a contract to that effect when they were two or three years old. But Anne started backsliding into faith at an early age. "Even when I was a child I knew that when I said Hello, someone heard."

Some people seem to have a kind of inner radar for detecting the presence of God. Just as certain musicians have perfect pitch, these people have an ear for discerning God's voice. They seem to be as aware of God as they are of gravity. Telling them how to look for God would be like telling a fish how to look for water—where else could they live?

But I am Adam. I believe my life hinges on the presence of God. I know that courage and guidance and hope all reside with him. But I am aware of the gap—even if it is only a hairbreadth. And in the midst of all my ambiguity—my weakness and occasional spiritual indifference—I long for the touch that will close the gap.

Dallas Willard (who lost his mother as a young child) writes of a little boy whose mom had died. He was especially sad and lonely at night. He would come into his father's room and ask if he could sleep with him. Even then he could not rest until he knew not only that he was with his father but that his father's face was turned toward him. "Father, is your face turned toward me now?" Yes, his father would say. You are not alone. I'm with you. My face is turned toward you. When at last he was assured of this, he could rest. Dallas goes on: "How lonely life is! Oh, we can get by in life with a God who does not speak. Many at least think they do so. But it is not much of a life, and it is certainly not the life God intends for us or the *abundance* of life Jesus came to make available."

> *I'm aware of the gap—even if it is only a hairbreadth. And I long for the touch that will close the gap.*

I want to live with God's face toward me. I want to experience—in the dark of night as well as the light of day—the reality that Moses prayed for: "The LORD bless you and keep you; the LORD make his face to shine upon you."

GOD WITH JACOB

Who is a candidate for such a life? Saints and mystics, of course; the devoted and the wise. But not just them. The candidates also include people who are chronically unsatisfied. Restless people and demanding people; whiners and complainers; the impossible to please.

Consider what happened to Jacob. He was no spiritual giant. His dad never cared for him much because, according to Meyers-Briggs, he had an INFP temperament and liked to hang around indoors. His dad preferred his other son, Esau, who, while not the brightest bulb on the chandelier and having a serious body hair problem, was a jock with hunter-gatherer potential.

One night Jacob was running away from Esau, who was trying to kill him because Jacob had cheated him and deceived their father. Jacob stopped for the night at "a certain place." That's a Hebrew way of saying no place in particular. Cleveland, maybe. It could have been anywhere. Some spot by the side of the road with nothing special about it.

Jacob had done nothing to merit what was about to happen to him. He had been a passive codependent of his mother's schemes, a jealous rival to his brother, and a brazen liar to his father.

But that night Jacob had a dream. He saw a ladder "resting on the earth, with its top reaching to heaven, and the angels of God were ascending and descending on it." God said to him:

> "I am the LORD, the God of your father Abraham and the God of Isaac.... I am *with* you and will watch over you wherever you go...."

> When Jacob awoke from his sleep, he thought, "Surely the LORD is in this place, and I was not aware of it.... This is none other than the house of God, this is the gate of heaven."

There is more than one form of sleep. Sometimes we are awakened by blessing: the birth of a baby, an unexplained healing; a marriage that was headed for divorce getting turned around. Sometimes we are awakened by suffering: God would later reveal himself again to Jacob by wrestling with him and dislocating his hip. The soul is pierced by beauty and suffering. But each moment that we live outside the awareness of God's presence is a kind of sleepwalking, which is why Paul wrote, "Wake up, O sleeper, rise from the dead, and Christ will shine on you." Somebody's eyes get opened to the fact that God is right here in this ordinary place, with this ordinary person.

The striking phrase of Jacob is "and I was not aware of it." Somehow he was looking in the wrong direction. Apparently it is possible for God to be present without the person recognizing that he is there. Apparently it is possible that God is closer than you think.

This is Jacob's discovery.

Jacob calls this place where he had the dream "Beth-el," that is, "the house of God, the place where God is present." It is transformed for him from "a certain place" — nowhere special — to the place inhabited by God himself.

WE *AREN'T* CLIMBING JACOB'S LADDER

We used to sing a song about this story in the church where I grew up: "We are climbing Jacob's ladder.... Every round goes higher, higher...." But the song gets the story wrong. It's not a ladder for human beings to climb *up*. It's a ladder for God to come *down*. All the way down to where we live.

This is the story of the God of the Sistine Chapel. God is still in the business of coming down to earth: to this cubicle, this email, this room, this house, this job, this hospital room, this car, this bed, this vacation. Any place can become Bethel, the house of God. Cleveland, maybe. Or the chair you're sitting in as you read these words.

Jacob's life starts to change, but not all at once. God's presence does not mean he is exempt from problems or character flaws. Yet his journey has begun. Eventually he decides to take the enormous risk of reconciling with his brother; instead of ripping him off, he wants to give back to him. He sends on ahead extravagant gifts: 220 goats, 220 ewes and rams, 30 camels, 50 cows and bulls, 30 donkeys, and a cat. (Actually, there is no cat in the story. The cat is not a biblical animal. Apparently even God doesn't like cats.)

Jacob sees his brother after two decades of separation and hatred. We wait to see whether Esau will kill him. "But Esau ran to meet Jacob and embraced him; he threw his arms around his neck and kissed him. And they wept."

Once you see God in an ordinary moment at an ordinary place, you never know where he'll show up next.

After a whole childhood of living as enemies, and two decades of living as strangers—now they are brothers. And Jacob makes one of the great statements of Scripture: "To see your face is *like seeing the face of God....*"

Because once you meet God at Bethel—

Once you see God in an ordinary moment at an ordinary place, you never know where he'll show up next. You could start seeing him anywhere—even in the face of someone who's been your mortal enemy for twenty years.

God is closer than you think....

GOD WAVING HELLO

My favorite author writes,

I have been asked by some how I can be so certain in the existence of a good God, and I have asked them in return if they have eyes to see. God has woven himself irretrievably into Nature; left his fingerprints behind to show us where he's been. His signature is smeared into the curls of the Milky Way, forever circling above the rim of the world. God has scattered fragments of himself all about the earth like a father hides eggs in the yard before his son's very first Easter; hiding behind a tree with laughing eyes and waiting to see which of the treasures his child will uncover first.

God is crying out all around us. He is present in the breathless silence of the snow-smothered mountains; he is dancing with the sunlight that shatters on the ocean's waves; he is hiding in the decaying moss and lichen and crumbling shale in the old forgotten places in the world. No jagged mountain throws its sharp weight against the sky that is not a testament to his goodness. The entire sum of Creation, each private and individual act of nature, is God waving hello.

In a city called Dothan, a servant of the prophet Elisha was terrified because he and his boss were surrounded by Israel's enemies. "What shall we do?" he cried. Elisha told him to chill out, for "those who are with us are more than those who are with them." Then he prayed for him: "O LORD, open his eyes so he may see." And the Lord opened his eyes, and he saw that he was surrounded by horses and chariots of fire — the power and protection of God.

What if this were to become your prayer as well? What if every time you are challenged or burdened, you too are surrounded by his power and protection? And what if God should open your eyes?

In the temple, in the night, a young boy named Samuel heard his named called out. He thought it was the priest, Eli, and kept running into his bedroom. Finally Eli realized that it was God speaking to

Samuel, but Samuel did not yet recognize God's voice. So Eli instructed him that the next time he heard the voice he should assume it was from God. He should invite God to speak further—and then be ruthlessly obedient.

What if God were to have the "ministry of Eli" to you? What if God has been speaking to you, calling your name—only you didn't know it?

Two early followers of Jesus were walking on the road to Emmaus after the crucifixion. They were joined by a third man. It was Jesus, walking and talking with them—but they didn't know it was he. Until he began to pray. And then they knew. And then they said, "Didn't our hearts burn within us as he explained the Scripture to us?"

What if when you are on the road to Emmaus—maybe the road on which you commute to work or school or home—Jesus is walking beside you? What if you join the "fellowship of the burning heart" and actually experience his presence?

HOW CLOSE HAS GOD COME?

Frederick Buechner writes, "There is no event so commonplace but that God is present within it, always hiddenly, always leaving you room to recognize him or not ... because in the last analysis all moments are key moments, and life itself is grace."

How close has God come? So close that, as Thomas à Kempis put it, "every creature will be to you a mirror of life and a book of holy doctrine." So close that, in the words of Jean Pierre de Caussade, "each moment is a revelation from God." So close that he can flow in and through your life from one moment to the next like a river. So close that your heart will be beating with life because Someone is walking around in there. God is closer than you think.

Set aside for now the question of to what extent any of us is capable of experiencing God's presence in our current spiritual condition. Set aside your past failures or future worries.

The teaching of Scripture is that God really is present right here, right now. Michelangelo's picture really does express spiritual reality. The Spirit of God is available to you and me: flowing all the time, welling up within us, quenching our unsatisfied desires, overflowing to refresh those around us. He is at work all the time, in every place. And every once in a while, somebody somewhere wakes up.

GOD WITH THE KITCHEN GUY

There are real people who claim it has happened before. It happened to a man named Nicholas Herman in the food service industry. He had had stints in the military and in transportation, and now he was a short-order cook and bottle-washer. But he became deeply dissatisfied with his life; he worried chronically about himself, even whether or not he was saved.

One day Nick was looking at a tree, and the same truth struck him that struck the psalmist so long ago: the secret of the life of a tree is that it remains rooted in something other and deeper than itself. He decided to make his life an experiment in what he called a "habitual, silent, secret conversation of the soul with God."

He is known today by the new name given to him by his friends: Brother Lawrence. He remained obscure throughout his life. He never got voted pope. He never got close to becoming the CEO of his organization. He stayed in the kitchen. But the people around him found that rivers of living water flowed out of him that made them want to know God the way he did. "The good brother found God everywhere," one of them wrote, "as much while he was repairing shoes as while he was praying with the community." After Lawrence died, his friends put together a book of his letters and conversations. It is called *Practicing the Presence of God* and is thought, apart from the Bible, to be the most widely read book of the last four centuries. This monastic short-order cook has probably out-sold novelists John Grisham and Tom Clancy and J. K. Rowling put together.

GOD WITH THE PROFESSOR

The offer of this *with-God* life has not expired in our day. When my friend Kim was a young girl, her dad pulled the car off the road one day to help a woman change a flat tire. While he was lying under her car, another vehicle accidentally swerved to the shoulder, and in the collision the car was shoved onto his chest. His right thumb was torn off at the joint, five of his ribs were broken, and his left lung was pierced and began filling with blood. His wife, who is barely five feet tall, placed her hands on the bumper of the car and prayed, "In the name of the Lord Jesus Christ," and lifted the car off his chest so he could be dragged out. (Some weeks later she found out that she broke a vertebra in the effort.)

Kim's father was in a state of shock as he was taken to the hospital. Doctors prepared for emergency surgery. "His thumb won't do him any good if he's dead," one of them said. His survival was iffy.

Suddenly, spontaneously, the man's skin changed from ashen to pink. He experienced a miraculous healing. He invited a surprised surgical team to join him in singing "Fairest Lord Jesus." They did not even bother to hook him up to oxygen. He did not find out until later that this was the precise moment his father-in-law, who was a pastor, had his congregation start to pray for him.

Sometimes these stories come from not-very-credible sources —such as publications sold in grocery checkout lines that also carry news about extraterrestrial creatures secretly playing third base for the Boston Red Sox. In this case, however, the subject was James Loder, a professor at Princeton Theological Seminary. His life was not only saved, but changed. Until then, although he taught at a seminary, God had been mostly an abstract idea to him. Now Jesus became a living Presence. Kim writes that her father's heart grew so tender that he became known at Princeton as "the weeping professor." He began to live from one moment to the next in a God-bathed, God-soaked, God-intoxicated world.

NOW IT'S OUR TURN

Spiritual growth, in a sense, is simply increasing our capacity to experience the presence of God. Brother Lawrence wrote, "The most holy and necessary practice in our spiritual life is the presence of God. That means finding constant pleasure in His divine company, speaking humbly and lovingly with him in all seasons, at every moment, without limiting the conversation in any way."

What if God could be that close? Maybe I miss him because I fail to see him in the ordinary moments of my life. Maybe every heartbeat is not just the mechanism of a sophisticated plumbing system but the echo of God's voice, the murmur of God's love. There are people — saints and mystics — who seem to find God in their lives as easily as the morning newspaper. They check their hearts and feel him walking around in there.

Spiritual growth, in a sense, is simply increasing our capacity to experience the presence of God.

No one has ever lived with a sense of the presence of God as Jesus did. He was so dependent on God that he said that everything he did was a result of God's power. He was so surrendered to God that he said his greatest delight was to do the will of his Father. He was so confident of God that neither stormy seas nor hostile crowds could shake his poise. The river of life flowed strong through this man Jesus as it had never flowed through anyone before him. And when he died, the veil that kept people out of the Holy of Holies — the veil that symbolized separation between God and human beings — was torn in two. In Jesus, God touched Adam.

Now, according to the clear expectation of the teaching of Jesus, it's our turn. What happened to a con man named Jacob, what happened to a servant of Elisha and a young boy named Samuel and a couple of discouraged disciples on the road to Emmaus, what happened to Brother Lawrence in a kitchen in France and James Loder in a hospital room can happen again.

The expectation of Jesus was that this unseen river of life will flow again: in an office in San Francisco, a home in the suburbs of Atlanta, at a desk in a classroom in Chicago. It can happen for an attendant working at a gas station in Detroit. It can happen for plumbers and stockbrokers and homemakers and retired folks. It can happen for CEOs and seventh graders. It can happen in Cleveland. It can flow through the life of a young, single mom with all the demands of raising young children. It can surge in a hospital bed where a solitary individual lies in the valley of the shadow of death.

FOUNDATIONAL TRUTHS OF MY LIFE WITH GOD

- God is always present and active in my life, whether or not I see him.
- Coming to recognize and experience God's presence is *learned* behavior; I can cultivate it.
- My task is to meet God in *this* moment.
- I am always tempted to live "outside" this moment. When I do that, I lose my sense of God's presence.
- Sometimes God seems far away for reasons I do not understand. Those moments, too, are opportunities to learn.
- Whenever I fail, I can always start again right away.
- No one knows the full extent to which a human being can experience God's presence.
- My desire for God ebbs and flows, but his desire for me is constant.
- Every thought carries a "spiritual charge" that moves me a little closer to or a little farther from God.
- Every aspect of my life—work, relationships, hobbies, errands—is of immense and genuine interest to God.
- My path to experiencing God's presence will not look quite like anyone else's.
- Straining and trying too hard do not help.

Review these truths once a day for two weeks as you cultivate the practice of God's presence.

It can happen for you. At the end of this chapter are some guiding principles for practicing God's presence. I would encourage you to read them each morning for the next two weeks as you make your own experiment in this "with-God" kind of life.

For centuries now, people have stood in line to view the picture of God and Adam on the ceiling of the Sistine Chapel. But what if the miracle that is hinted at on that fresco became a reality in our lives?

What if an artist greater than Michelangelo is at work on the canvas of our ordinary days? "God alone is capable of making himself known as he really is," Brother Lawrence said. "God Himself paints Himself in the depths of our souls."

It can happen anywhere, anytime, for anyone. Whatever your age or season of life or temperament or job—these are no obstacle at all. All you have to do is lift a finger. God is closer than you think.

CHAPTER 2

WHERE'S WALDO?

*We may ignore, but we cannot evade, the presence of God. The
world is crowded with him. He walks everywhere incognito. And
the incognito is not always easy to penetrate. The real labor is to
remember to attend.*

Armand Nicholi

On Michelangelo's ceiling, all Adam has to do is lift a finger
and he can touch the hand of God. God is that close. This is
the teaching of Scripture. This is the faith I have committed myself
to. Yet it's not that simple—not for me, anyway. Sometimes I wish
God would show himself more plainly, maybe come down from the
clouds every once in a while and part Lake Michigan so I could see for
myself. He is, after all, invisible, inaudible, and untouchable. None of
my other friends possess these qualities, and it would make relating to
them much harder if they did. Sometimes I lift a finger; sometimes I
really do try, but not much seems to happen.

When I teach on this subject, these are the questions that arise
most frequently:

— "Why do I sometimes feel God's presence stronger in my daily
life than other times?"

— "When it is so easy to 'see' God all around me (in trees, in birds,
in nature), why is it so hard to feel his presence—especially
when I need him most?"

— "Why is it that at times when I seek God I feel no response? Am I asking amiss? How can I know?"

When I think about this subject, these are also the questions I most frequently ask myself.

So I remember another, humbler work of art. It involves a series of books all centered around the question "Where's Waldo?"

"SOMETIMES HE HIDES HIMSELF"

Waldo will never make it to the Sistine Chapel. He looks nothing like the majestic deity of Michelangelo. He is a geeky-looking, glasses-wearing nerd with a striped shirt and goofy hat.

Waldo was created by an illustrator named Martin Handford. He was just an afterthought initially; Handford wanted to draw crowd scenes. But children grew fascinated with trying to find their hero — so fascinated that more than 40 million "Where's Waldo" books have been sold in twenty-eight countries.

This guy Waldo is supposed to be on every page. The author assures us that it is so. But you couldn't prove it by me. He is often hidden to the untrained eye. You have to be willing to look for him. "Surely Waldo was in this place, and I knew it not."

When you find him, there is a sense of joy and accomplishment. In fact, developing the capacity to track him down is part of the point of the book. If it were too easy — if every page consisted just of a giant picture of Waldo's face — no one would ever buy the book. The difficulty of the task is what increases the power of discernment. The author said he hides Waldo so children can learn to "be aware of what's going on around them. I'd like them to see wonder in places it might not have occurred to them."

Part of what makes it hard to find Waldo is that he is so ordinary-looking.

But sometimes it takes a while to find Waldo. It demands patience. Some people are better at it than others. Some people just give up.

Part of what makes it hard to find Waldo is that he is so ordinary-looking. In the initial pages his presence is obvious. Later on, he's hidden but the other occupants of the page are giants and sea monsters, so Waldo still stands out. Then eventually we come to the last and hardest page. By the end he's in a room full of Waldos virtually identical to himself, the only distinction being that one detail is different, such as he's missing a shoe. Handford allows rival Waldos to counterfeit his identity. You can be looking right at him without even knowing it. Where's Waldo? Why doesn't he show himself plainly? Why does he hide his face? He may not be absent, but he is elusive. He is *Waldus absconditus*—the Waldo who hides himself.

Let every day, every moment, of your life be another page. God is there, the Scriptures tell us—on every one of them. But the ease with which he may be found varies from one page to the next. Brother Lawrence wrote, "God has various ways of drawing us to him, but sometimes he hides himself." So let's explore the Waldo factor.

RAINBOW DAYS

God is easy to find on some pages. "The LORD saw how great man's wickedness on the earth had become.... The LORD was grieved that he had made man on the earth, and his heart was filled with pain." The Lord told Noah that he had caught his eye, that he and his family were to be spared from coming destruction, to be the hope of the world. God said, "I will make a covenant with you and every living creature, from this time on. I will be with you. And I will give you a sign of my covenant: the rainbow."

And Noah said, "Wow!"

At least I'm guessing that he did. Every time he saw a rainbow in the sky, Noah remembered that he had God's promise. Every time he saw a rainbow, he knew he was not alone.

God must have been very clear that day. God must have been very present to Noah on rainbow days.

Skip down a few generations. One day God came to a man named Abraham. In a world filled with violence, he let Abraham know that he had caught the Lord's eye, that Abraham would become a blessing to the nations. Abraham would have to leave his home and everything familiar and go to a place that he did not know. But he would not have to do it alone. God said, "I will make a covenant with you. From this time on, you will be my people, and I will be your God. I will be with you. And I will give you a sign of my covenant: circumcision."

We can imagine Abraham replying, "Noah got the rainbow. Couldn't we use a decoder ring or a secret handshake or something?"

Abraham's day was a little more painful than Noah's. But it was unmistakable. God must have been very clear that day.

On rainbow days God's presence is hard to miss. On rainbow days the veil that separates the natural from the supernatural gets pretty thin. I have never had an experience like Noah's or Abraham's. I haven't witnessed a physical visitation. I haven't seen an empirically verifiable miracle. I've never had an experience of God that involved heaven's special effects department. But I have had some "thin places" at the fabric of my life.

When each of my three children was born, I was seized by the conviction that something more than just a blob of tissue had entered the world. I knew I had been invited to witness the supernatural. When I watched my children enter the world, I could not *not* believe. It was as if God himself were in the room. (Which may be why my wife said his name a lot during labor.) The births of my children were rainbow days.

On rainbow days your life is filled with too much goodness and meaning for you to believe it is simply by chance. On rainbow days you find yourself wanting to pray, believing that God hears, open to receiving and acting on his response. On rainbow days God seems to speak personally to you through Scripture. You find yourself believing that it is a good thing to be alive, and each good thing you see fills you with gratitude toward the God who made it. Sin doesn't even look tempting. When you're in this zone, the kids can spill gallons of red Kool-Aid on a white carpet and you laugh patiently and remind them that you often spilled things yourself when you were a child. In the words of the old song, it's

Summertime, and the livin' is easy;
Fish are jumpin' and the cotton is high.
Your daddy's rich and your mama's good lookin'....

RAINBOW DAYS ARE GIFTS

It can be easy to take rainbow days for granted or assume they will go on forever. But that's a big mistake. One of the best questions we can ask is what factors may have been contributing to a time of spiritual flourishing. I am writing these words early on a Monday morning. I am sitting in a ranch house perched on a hilltop, miles from noise, and watching the sun rise through one window and seeing the Pacific ocean through another. It's January, and the whales are swimming along the coast down to Baja on their annual winter break, like Canadians who have time-share condos in Florida.

Somehow I almost find it hard *not* to sense God's presence when I watch the sun come up in silence, or hear the waves of an ocean like those that broke on this shore thousands of years before my arrival on this planet and will still ebb and flow long after I am gone. There is something about a whale coming up for air that makes my heart beat a little faster. ("There is the sea, vast and spacious, teeming with creatures beyond number ... the leviathan, which you formed to frolic there.")

The house belongs to a friend of mine, and I am thinking about asking him to adopt me so I can wake up here every morning. I'm reminded of how much more open I am to God's presence when solitude and silence and immersion in creation are part of my life.

People who are wise learn to treasure rainbow days as gifts. They store them up to remember on days when God seems more elusive. One of the dangers in this, however, is that we may start to think we have earned them, that they are a reflection of our spiritual maturity. We can become judgmental toward people who don't have rainbow days.

As we have seen, the title character in Waldo books is generally easiest to find on the earliest pages. The farther you get into the book, the harder he is to locate. Something like this often goes on in spiritual life. St. John of the Cross wrote that often when someone first becomes a Christian God fills them with a desire to seek him: They want to read Scripture, they are eager to pray, they are filled with a desire to serve. These characteristics are, in a sense, gifts from God to get them moving; a kind of spiritual starter kit. After a while, John of the Cross said, this initial eagerness wears off. God takes away the props so that we can begin to grow true devotion that is strong enough to carry on even when unaided by emotions.

> *People who are wise learn to store up rainbow days to remember on days when God seems more elusive.*

ORDINARY DAYS

During some eras of spiritual life we fall into a kind of maintenance mode. Life becomes routine. At this time there is not a major crisis, no obvious problems, but no major gains either. We feel somewhat comfortable.

Our involvement in the life of the church is kind of mechanical. We may feel as if we're in a bit of a spiritual rut. If we're honest about it, we're a little bored. We do not experience being in the flow with God. When problems crop up, our instinctive response is to worry rather than pray. When we wake up, our first thoughts are more apt to go toward the burden of all we have to do today rather than the excitement of God's promise to partner with us. When the kids spill Kool-Aid on the carpet, we're not so perky.

Waldo is still present on these pages of our lives. We can find him, if we remember to look. But we're apt not to notice him. Our attention is elsewhere.

There is a fascinating line in 1 Samuel that describes the condition of Israel in the waning days of the era of the judges. Many of the challenges that made the people aware of their dependence on God are behind them. Pharaoh is long since defeated, the Ten Commandments and Mount Sinai are old news, and manna is a collector's item. The exciting era of Moses and Joshua is over. The miracle of the Exodus is complete, the burden of occupying new ground is finished, people have settled into the land God had promised them. And the writer describes the spiritual climate with these words: "In those days, the word of the LORD was rare."

Rare, but not nonexistent. The people are not in a state of major rebellion. The tabernacle is still open for worship, prayers are still offered, and sacrifices are still made. But this is not a time of great spiritual adventure. God may be present, but people aren't thinking of him quite as often as they did when the Jordan was being parted. The heavens may still be declaring the glory of God, but the people are channel surfing.

Sometimes it is rare for us, too.

SPIRITUAL HABITUATION

Psychologists who deal with the study of perception refer to a phenomenon called "habituation." The idea is that when a new object or stimulus is introduced to our environment, we are intensely aware of it, but the awareness fades over time. So, for instance, when we first begin to wear a new wristwatch, we feel it on our wrist constantly, but after a while we don't even notice that it's there.

When people move into a new home, they generally have a list of things they *must* repair or remodel because the sight of them is intolerable. Five years later, they may still have the same list, but the lack of repair doesn't bother them anymore.

> *Spiritual habituation is in some ways more dangerous than spiritual depravity because it can be so subtle, so gradual.*

Years ago we had a dog that used to eat our furniture. When I say "eat," I don't mean "chew on." He ate the top off the ottoman in front of our sofa so that the foam rubber was exposed, then he ate most of the foam rubber. The pathetic part is, we got used to a half-eaten, foam-rubber-exposed ottoman. After a while we didn't even notice it anymore. We habituated.

One of the greatest challenges in life is fighting what might be called spiritual habituation. We simply drift into acceptance of life in spiritual maintenance mode. We rationalize it because we think, "I'm not involved in major scandalous sin. I haven't done anything to jeopardize getting into heaven. I'm doing okay." And we forget that Jesus never said, "I have come that you might do okay." Okay is not okay. We have a kind of spiritual attention deficit disorder that God will have to break through.

When life is on spiritual autopilot, rivers of living water do not flow through it with energy and joy. Instead it looks like this:

— I yell at my children.

— I worry too much about money or my job.

— I get jealous of people more successful or attractive than I.

— I use deception to get out of trouble.

— I pass judgment on people, often when I am secretly jealous of them.

Spiritual habituation is in some ways more dangerous than spiritual depravity because it can be so subtle, so gradual. Mostly it involves a failure to see.

We are drawn to children and saints and poets because they *notice* things that the rest of us have forgotten to see. "I hold this against you," Jesus said to the church at Ephesus. "You have forsaken your first love."

We saw in chapter 1 that God sent Jacob a dream at Bethel. So why doesn't he send us all dreams every night? Why doesn't he make every day a rainbow day and send epiphanies twenty-four-seven? Maybe it's because God wants us to learn to see him in the ordinary rather than be dependent on the extraordinary. Maybe it's because if God regularly satisfied our demand for special effects it would be like a mother who inadvertently trains her children to pay attention only when she raises her voice.

Nancy and I have discovered a strange parenting phenomenon. When we raise the volume level to get our children's attention, they pretty quickly tune us out. But when we lower our voices to speak about something private with each other (birthday presents, maybe, or modes of punishment), our kids become instantly attentive. Words we try to whisper will be heard three rooms and two closed doors away. It is as if our children have an inner instinct for when we are trying to keep information from them and suddenly develop auditory abilities that CIA operatives would pay for.

Maybe the reason God lowers his voice is so we will learn to pay attention. Maybe it is an invitation to become like one of the characters in the novel *The Prince of Tides*, about whom the narrator says,

> I would like to have walked his world, thanking God for oysters and porpoises, praising God for birdsong and sheet lightning, seeing God reflected in pools of creekwater and the eyes of stray cats. I would like to have talked to yard dogs as if they were my friends and fellow travelers along the sun-tortured highways intoxicated with the love of God. . . . *I would like to have seen the whole world with eyes incapable of anything but wonder, and with a tongue fluent only in praise.*

Maybe ordinary days aren't "ordinary" at all, but part of the required course to develop wonder-filled eyes and praise-fluent tongues. William Barry writes, "Whether we are aware of it or not, at every moment of our existence we are encountering God, Father, Son, and Holy Spirit, who is trying to catch our attention, trying to draw us into a reciprocal conscious relationship." Perhaps our capacity to pay attention to God — like the capacity to lift weights or speak Spanish — only gets stronger when it gets exercised.

REVIEWING THE DAILIES

A filmmaking technique teaches us a way to see God in the ordinary. A cinematographer, Bob Fisher, wrote a passionate article recently about the need for movie crews to spend some time every day reviewing the film that was shot the day before. By delaying production temporarily to review the previous day's work, filmmakers can spot little mistakes while they can still be corrected and can celebrate what is going right. In Fisher's words, "Watching film dailies is uplifting. It energizes everyone."

In a similar way, it's a very helpful thing for us to take a few moments to "review the dailies" with God. You can do this right now by walking through yesterday in your mind with God and asking where he was present and at work in each scene. Start with the moment when you woke up in the morning. God was present, waking you up, giving you a mini-resurrection. What were your first thoughts? What do you think God wanted to say to you in that moment?

Then go on from one scene to the next through your day. As I review what happened when I greeted my family, ate breakfast, and went through meetings at work, I see patterns emerging—the ongoing presence of anxiety or anger—that I miss when I don't take time to review the dailies. Most of all, I look and listen to see how God is speaking to me through these scenes. I realize he was talking to me through the words of another person or the lines of a book or the therapy of laughter. The more often I review, the better I get at recognizing him in "real time."

Many times I have led a group of people to take five minutes to do this exercise. At the end I often ask those who found something to be thankful for in the previous day to raise their hands. Everyone raises a hand. We find that ordinary days had little rainbow moments in them.

SPIRITUAL HIDING

Sometimes we don't have much of a sense for God's presence in our lives, but there's no mystery to it at all. The truth is that our desire for God can be pretty selective. Sometimes we don't *want* God to be around.

Dallas Willard writes about a two-and-a-half-year-old girl in the backyard who one day discovered the secret to making mud (which she called "warm chocolate"). Her grandmother had been reading and was facing away from the action, but after cleaning up what was to her a mess, she told little Larissa not to make any more chocolate and turned her chair around so as to be facing her granddaughter.

The little girl soon resumed her "warm chocolate" routine, with one request posed as sweetly as a two-and-a-half-year-old can make it: "Don't look at me, Nana. Okay?"

Nana (being a little codependent) of course agreed.

Larissa continued to manufacture warm chocolate. Three times she said, as she continued her work, "Don't look at me, Nana. Okay?"

Then Willard writes, "Thus the tender soul of a little child shows us how necessary it is to us that we be unobserved in our wrong."

Any time we choose to do wrong or to withhold doing right, we choose hiddenness as well. It may be that out of all the prayers that are ever spoken, the most common one—the quietest one, the one that we least acknowledge making—is simply this:

Don't look at me, God.

It was the very first prayer spoken after the Fall. God came to walk in the garden, to be with the man and the woman, and called, "Where are you?"

"I heard you in the garden, and I was afraid, ... so I hid."

Don't look at me, God.

A businessman on the road checks into a motel room late at night. He knows the kind of movies that are available to him in the room. No one will know. His wife won't find out; his kids won't see. (The motel has a disclaimer: "The name of movie you watch won't be on your bill. Go ahead. No one will know.") First he has to say a little prayer: "Don't look at me, God."

> *It may be that the most common prayer—the one that we least acknowledge making—is simply this: Don't look at me, God.*

A mom with an anger problem decides to berate her kids because she's so frustrated, because she will get a twisted rush of pleasure from inflicting pain. First she has to say a little prayer: "Don't look at me, God."

An executive who's going to pad an expense account—

An employee who is going to deliberately make a coworker look bad—

A student who looks at somebody else's paper during an exam—

A church member who looks forward to the chance to gossip—
First must say a little prayer.

We don't say it out loud, of course. We probably don't admit it even to ourselves. But it's the choice our heart makes:

Don't look at me, God.

After a while this prayer can become so ingrained that we're not even aware of it. The story of Samson is the tale of the man with enormous potential for good who became a poster boy for impulse control problems that led him to break every vow he had ever made to God. At the end of his life comes this sad sentence: "But he did not know that the LORD had left him."

There is a connection between our character and our ability to perceive spiritual and moral reality. Misers are incapable of detecting generosity in someone; they will interpret lavish giving as naiveté or secretly self-serving. Cynics are incapable of believing anyone is genuinely altruistic; they will assume everyone has an angle.

THE LAW OF THE OATMEAL BRUSH

Sin always has the consequence of damaging our ability to perceive God in the present moment. Consider, for example, the Law of the Oatmeal Brush.

For some years I have been trying to make each day an adventure in practicing God's presence. I try to direct my thoughts toward him first thing when I wake up in the morning. On one particular morning I was getting ready to leave for work. I'd had oatmeal for breakfast, and after I finished washing my dishes, the white scrub brush in our sink was covered with oatmeal.

My wife asked me, "Are you done with this brush? If you are, it'd be helpful to just whack it on the sink, get oatmeal stuff out."

I was feeling defensive. I had actually been kind of proud of myself for washing the dishes in the first place. I didn't want someone telling me to clean the oatmeal brush.

So what I said was, "No, I'm not done with it." The reality is that the dishes were done. What was I pretending I was going to do with it? Brush the oatmeal junk into my hair? It wasn't just a lie—it was an unbelievably *stupid* lie. Even *I* couldn't pretend I believed it for a second.

But as long as I tried to maintain it, a strange dynamic was at work in my spirit. I had to muster up enough anger and hurt and pride to justify my deceit. I had to cut myself off from humility and truth. I had to say the prayer, "Don't look at me, God."

And as soon as I confessed the ridiculous truth to my wife, I could quit hiding. I could see Waldo on the page again. *The Law of the Oatmeal Brush is that every choice to sin — no matter how small — diminishes my capacity to experience God.* Now, every morning when I see the Oatmeal Brush, it has become a kind of icon for me. It reminds me how quickly I can go into hiding.

WHEN GOD SEEMS AWOL

But now we come to the hardest condition. Sometimes I cannot find Waldo no matter how hard I try. Sometimes it seems that God cannot be found even though we really want to find him.

I have had times when I tried to pray — really tried — and the ceiling in my room seemed like the barrier my prayers bounced off of. I think about times I've had an important decision to make: telling God I'd do whatever he wanted if he would just tell me what to do. And I heard nothing. I think of days when I have carried a ball of anxiety in my belly; asking God to send peace, yet the pain remained.

And it's not just me.

A young girl named Nancy was in a romantic relationship that she was quite sure would end in marriage, only it didn't. She prayed, and God didn't answer; she got mad and got no response; she was sad and lost twenty pounds and got no comfort. This era didn't last forever. But for a long time it was hard to see God in the picture. (Eventually she gave up on that relationship, and still later she married me, so I like to think the story had a happy ending.).

Sometimes a story is more dramatic. I think of another friend of mine, one of the smartest men I've ever known. We went to the same college and grad school. I'm not sure I know anybody who has read more about God or thought more about faith than he has. In the space of a few years, through a sad chain of events he lost his marriage, his home, his financial well-being, and his career. He was left with a single consolation: a daughter whom he loved, who doted on his every word. She was smart like her dad. Before she was even old enough to go to school they read through *The Lord of the Rings* together; she knew all the characters. When he had lost everything else, she was the sun around which his little world orbited. One day on vacation with relatives she was on a carriage ride. Crossing a stream, the horses spooked and reared up, she was thrown into the current. It took hours before they found her body. Now he had lost everything. Now he had to ask where God is when something as precious as the life of a child is lost through such a freak roll of the cosmic dice.

A young man I know came from a very unsafe family that was both violent and sexually abusive. His conversion to friendship with Jesus five years ago was a remarkable thing to see. To anyone watching him, he is a model of faithfulness. He is very active at church and well disciplined in his devotional habits. He witnesses often to others and can argue eloquently for his faith. But his discipline masks a deep-seated fear that he will never really experience God. He is secretly thinking of converting to Judaism because it doesn't emphasize as much a personal relationship with God.

THE GOOD OF NOT KNOWING

The sense of God's hiddenness is so important that we will spend a whole chapter looking at it in more detail. For now I want to suggest that perhaps in his hiddenness, too, God is up to something. George MacDonald wrote a book about a pastor named Thomas Wingfold, who is troubled by doubt and his inability to *know* God is present. He decides to make his life an experiment in seeking simply to follow Jesus in spite of his doubts. At one point he is caring for a dying man who has come to faith through his influence. "I wish I could come back after I die, " the man tells Wingfold, "so you could be delivered from doubts and know *for sure* about the faith."

Then Wingfold says the words that have stayed with me ever since. "No—even if you could, I wouldn't want you to. I would not see him one moment before he thought best. I'd rather have *the good of not knowing.*"

It had never occurred to me before that there might be a reason for uncertainty—a good of not knowing. I thought of this line again years later when my daughter came into my room. She had applied to college and was desperate to find out if she had gotten in to her top choice. It struck me, as we talked, that the "uncertainty period" was a unique opportunity for growth. If she were able to live with confidence and joy even when she did not yet know if she'd get what she hoped for, a kind of strength would be formed in her soul that would never get formed there if she found out the answer right away. There is a good of not knowing.

I heard a radio interview sometime ago with Marv Levy, who coached the Buffalo Bills to four consecutive Super Bowl appearances —all of which they lost. The interviewer asked him, "How did you handle the uncertainty of walking onto the field and not knowing the outcome? How did you manage the anxiety?"

Levy's answer was unforgettable. "If you're looking for certainty," he said, "you've chosen the wrong game." It's one of the differences between going to a Super Bowl and going to a theater. Everybody knows Hamlet's going to die.

> *Not knowing doesn't mandate anxiety; rather, it instills confidence, and confidence is crucial to good performance.*

But imagine for a moment two football teams walking onto the field knowing ahead of time what the final score of the game is going to be. It would be very hard to get much adrenaline going. Not knowing doesn't mean you're condemned to anxiety; rather, not knowing calls for trust, and trust is crucial to good performance. Uncertainty is essential to the game.

Welcome to the human race. It is somehow essential to human life as God has ordained it that we can know the final score of yesterday but not tomorrow. It doesn't mean we're condemned to anxiety. It does mean this:

If you're looking for certainty, you've chosen the wrong species. You can walk by faith, but not by sight; not down here.

Maybe this is why we must struggle with the not-knowing times of life. Thomas Merton once said that if you find God with great ease, perhaps it is not God that you have found.

Brother Lawrence himself said that when he first decided to pursue God's presence above all else, he was not very good at it. "It seemed that everything—even God (!)—was against me and that only faith was on my side." This sense of chronic failure lasted ten years. "When I finally reached the point where I expected the rest of my life to be very difficult, I suddenly found myself changed."

GOD WHERE YOU LEAST EXPECT HIM

You have to trust the author. You have to believe that God has a good reason for keeping his presence subtle. It allows creatures as small and frail as human beings the capacity for choice that we would never have in the obvious presence of infinite power. People driving behind a police car don't speed—not always because their hearts are right, but because they don't want to get pulled over.

God wants to be known, but not in a way that overwhelms us, that takes away the possibility of love freely chosen. "God is like a person who clears his throat while hiding and so gives himself away," said Meister Eckhart.

You never know where he'll turn up, or whom he'll speak through, or what unlikely scenario he'll use for his purpose. After the resurrection, Mary Magdalene was looking right at Jesus but thought he was the landscaping service guy.

God is often present, the Bible says, but apparently he often shows up in unexpected ways. He travels incognito. He is the master of disguise.

The image of God that Michelangelo created became famous. Probably, when people try to picture God in their minds, that image is the largest single influence in the world. It speaks something of the kind of majesty and dignity and strength we associate with the God of the Universe.

But when God did come down to be with us—*Immanuel*—he did not look like that. It's as if he put on Waldo's goofy-looking glasses and a striped shirt. He looked ordinary. He had no "majesty," that we should be attracted to him. He was weak enough that he was called "despised and rejected by men."

So God came down and was born in a manger and got a job in the construction industry pounding nails eight hours a day. God was on every page, but no one recognized him, because everyone was expecting somebody who looked like the guy we see on the ceiling of the Sistine Chapel.

Where's Waldo? He's right around the corner. He's lurking where you least expect him. He's right there on the page. He's anywhere people are willing to see the whole world with eyes incapable of anything but wonder, and with a tongue fluent only in praise.

He's closer than you think. So come with me to the next chapter. It's time to close the gap.

CHAPTER 3

LIFE WITH GOD

Who [in the Bible] besides Jesus really knew which end was up?
Nobody.... Jesus realized there is no separation from God.

J. D. Salinger

Until recently my wife headed up a ministry that involved about fifteen hundred young adults, which meant that she was surrounded by hundreds of men in their twenties. This had several implications for my life. One was that I had to keep myself in superb physical condition. Another was that I learned a lot more about postmodern relating patterns than I otherwise would have.

One of the staples of such patterns is a conversation known as a D.T.R.

You most likely know what this is if you're under thirty. The letters stand for "Define the Relationship." It generally gets used in relationships between a man and a woman that have romantic overtones but are squishy about permanence and exclusivity. It is a clarion call for relational clarity: Are we in this relationship for laughs, or are we in it for keeps?

Its usage in a sentence will go something like this: the person who wants a higher commitment level (otherwise known as the "DTR-er") will say to the commitment-squishy person (otherwise known as the "DTR-ee"), "I think it's time we had a little D.T.R." The very mention of those three letters will double the pulse rate of the DTR-ee because there is, of course, no such thing as a "little" D.T.R.

A SPIRITUAL D.T.R.

In Jesus' day, being in relationship with him inevitably involved having some spiritual D.T.R. Jesus was constantly calling for this in his relationships on earth. Nobody ever went away from an encounter with Jesus saying, "That was a good talk."

Jesus gently but relentlessly asked people to make a decision about their relationship with him. The fundamental decision involved this invitation: Follow me. Come be with me, and learn from me how to be like me.

Now it's our day. Jesus has promised that he and his Father will come and make their home in us, if that is what we want. For our part, the adventure of living in the presence of Jesus begins with a single decision. It can be expressed in the form of an ancient prayer (which we will see later in this chapter). We will learn to pray it over and over—at the beginning of the day, the end of the day, and a hundred times in between.

Jesus himself called this decision choosing "the one thing needful." To learn about this decision, we will look at some D.T.R. he had with a woman named Martha.

IT'S NOT ABOUT PERSONALITY TYPES

Jesus is staying on this particular occasion with Martha and her sister, Mary. Mary sits at his feet to learn from him, but Martha works in the kitchen and complains that she's not getting any help. She's in the same house with him, but they're worlds apart. She has proximity, but not intimacy.

> "Martha, Martha," the Lord said, "you are worried and upset about many things, but only one thing is needed. Mary has chosen what is better, and it will not be taken away from her."

This story is often misunderstood, I think, to be about two different personality types.

The Mary type is thought to be quiet, reflective, deep. This type has a strong natural pull toward the value of stillness. These people agree with Socrates that "the unexamined life is not worth living."

They cherish clarity and serenity. They like to ponder great thoughts; they want to experience life with mindfulness and depth.

The Martha type, by contrast, is busy, active, achievement-oriented. If you are a multitasker, Martha is your patron saint. What she is doing in the story—trying simultaneously to get a meal ready, get a house cleaned up, listen to spiritual teaching, and tell somebody else what to do—strikes you as the way life ought to be lived. If you're a Martha type, you're working on your grocery list in the margins of this book right now. Or more likely, you're listening to the audio version of this book while driving a car, checking voice messages at work on your cell phone, drinking a double espresso, and either shaving or applying lipstick.

This is a story about being with Jesus. But people often wrongly assume the story teaches that God's presence requires us to stop doing things. He's not into tasks. He's not into "to do" lists. It's better to sit quietly in the living room than work laboriously in the kitchen.

The story about Mary and Martha teaches something different from what many people think it does.

If you really want to practice the presence of God, according to this line of thought, you will have to cease all this striving and effort. Stop doing! Just be! If you're a Mary type, you are secretly glad any time this story gets retold. If you have a Martha in your life, you're already thinking about giving her this chapter to read, because you're thinking—in your own sweet, unhurried, contemplative way, "Now Martha's gonna get hers."

But there's a problem with this.

There are these pesky places in Scripture where Jesus has a lot to say about doing. Jesus often tells stories about workers. In one of them it is the high achiever who gets commended while the laid-back, passive man is called "wicked and lazy." In another story, a father says to his two sons, "Go and work in the vineyard." The son who decided, "I don't want to work; work is doing, I'm into being," doesn't come out so well.

Jesus said of himself, "My food is to do the will of him who sent me and to finish his work." He told us to pray that the Lord of the harvest would send workers into the field. The last thing he told his closest friends was to hit the road—go throughout the world, devoting themselves to making disciples and teaching them to do everything he commanded. That turned out to be a lot of work. And it would be precisely in that doing, Jesus promised, that "I will be with you always."

If the story in Luke shows that only the Mary type can really experience the full presence of Jesus—that it's better to sit quietly in the living room than be busy in the kitchen—then why are Jesus and his followers so often busy in the Gospels? To a mother with young children, words like stillness and solitude are elusive if not oxymorons: Can it really be God's plan that in their activity they should experience his presence less than a hermit in some cave?

This kind of thinking creates one of the great barriers to non-monks for practicing God's presence: the belief that my temperament or the demands and activity of my daily life inevitably interfere with my living in the presence of Jesus.

"SITTING AT THE LORD'S FEET"

Let's go deeper into the story about Mary and Martha, because its not really about personality types at all. It is D.T.R. conversation about a fundamental Decision, and a fundamental Obstacle. Both of them are crucial to anyone who wants to find Waldo on every page.

At the beginning of the story Luke says that Martha "opened her home to him." The implication is that he would be spending the night there. The obligation to provide hospitality in the Ancient Near East was very strong. There were no Motel 6's or Shalom Inns. Travelers were dependent on the hospitality of private homes.

Amazingly, Jesus is willing to be entertained in a home headed by an unmarried woman, Martha. And the home includes her unmarried sister, Mary. We tend to skip past this detail, but it would shock any first-century reader. This is unprecedented behavior for a rabbi in that day. It begins to explain a certain tension present in the story.

This tension is compounded by Luke's account of what Mary is doing: she "sat at the Lord's feet."

This is not just a description of her location in the room. And it certainly doesn't mean that Jesus wanted Mary to do nothing the rest of her life but sit around. It is an assertion that Mary has made the fundamental decision of her life. To "sit at someone's feet" was a technical expression in ancient times to indicate the relationship between a disciple and a rabbi. For instance, when Paul described his credentials to a Jewish crowd in Jerusalem he put it like this: "I am a Jew, born in Tarsus in Cilicia, but brought up in this city at the feet of Gamaliel, educated strictly...."

To make someone your rabbi was fundamentally a choice about being with him. A disciple was someone who had chosen to be with his rabbi as much as possible in order to learn everything he could from him.

Sitting "at the Lord's feet" is an assertion that Mary has made the fundamental decision of her life.

In ancient times, disciples would try to be around their rabbi everywhere and not just during formal teaching times. They wanted to see how their rabbi would handle money, what he would do if a woman tried to engage him in conversation. They would compete with each other to be with the rabbi when he was fixing meals, when he was doing chores, even when he was going to the bathroom(!), because they were concerned he might say a prayer that they had never heard. The ancient Talmud actually has a story about a disciple who snuck under his rabbi's bed so that he would be present when the rabbi and his wife went to bed with each other. He was discovered, and the rabbi wanted to know what his prize pupil was doing next to his slippers. His response was a classic: "This too is Torah, and I need to learn!" (In this case, his rabbi felt he had gone a little too far.) One ancient piece of instruction ran "Let your house be a meeting place for the sages, and sit in the very dust of their feet, and thirstily drink in their words."

"THE DUST OF YOUR RABBI"

Biblical scholar Ray van der Laan notes that the first-century Jews had a blessing that beautifully expresses the commitment of a disciple to stay in the presence of the one he followed: "May you always be covered by the dust of your rabbi." That is, "May you follow him so closely that the dust his feet kicks up is what cakes your clothing and lines your face." Like a baby duckling whose image of its mother has been imprinted on its brain, disciples never wanted to let the rabbi out of their sight. What mattered was not so much the particular activity they were doing. What mattered was being with their rabbi whatever was going on. Every activity was an opportunity to learn from the rabbi how to be like the rabbi. I can be "sitting at Jesus feet" when I'm kneeling in prayer or negotiating a contract or fixing my kids lunch or watching a movie. All it requires is my asking him to be my teacher and companion in this moment.

So let the letters D.T.R. take on one more meaning: "Dust of The Rabbi." That represents how Jesus invites us to define the relationship: to intend to live so much in his presence that we are dusty disciples.

This was the choice Mary had made. Jesus said "only one thing is needed," and that is the "one thing" that Mary had chosen, which would not be taken from her. The one thing was not that she would spend the rest of her life sitting in contemplation, letting Martha do all the work. The one thing was being with Jesus no matter what else was going on around her.

The decision that makes us disciples is choosing to be always with Jesus so we can learn continually from Jesus how to be fully like him.

Have you ever chosen the "one thing needed" in your life? What if you were to wake up each morning and begin with this prayer: "Today I would like to be covered in the dust of my rabbi"? What if you were to repeat that prayer all through the day every time it came to mind?

Maybe you think you're not qualified. So here is another detail we are apt to overlook, even though no one in the first century would.

Prior to Jesus, guess how many rabbis in all recorded history had a female disciple? Zero. No respectable rabbi would let a woman close enough to be covered with his dust. Until now. Jesus has made God's presence scandalously available to anyone who wants it. Male or female, young or old, hermit or homemaker, peasant or king: God is closer than you think.

THE FUNDAMENTAL OBSTACLE

Meanwhile, Martha is in the kitchen. Luke alerts us to the great obstacle that keeps us from being with Jesus when he says that Martha was "distracted" by all the preparations. Luke doesn't say she was too busy. He doesn't say she was over-committed. His word is "distracted"—a word sometimes used as meaning to be physically pulled or dragged away from something. The implication is that Martha had wanted to be with Jesus; that was her initial intent. But she allowed herself to be prevented from doing that by the pressure of providing hospitality. The question is, who said she had to provide this high level of hospitality?

It wasn't Jesus. Where did this voice come from that said, "You must do this"?

Maybe it was her culture. Maybe it was the stereotypical role of women. Maybe it was a little voice inside her head. Maybe it was her mom.

Maybe it was her reputation, what she was known for. Her name was from the Aramaic term "Mar" that was used for "mistress of the house," or hostess. Maybe that's what she was famous for—being "Martha." Maybe her last name was "Stewart."

She is in the kitchen. She doesn't have to be, and Jesus doesn't want her there, but there she is. She has a desire to be in the presence of Jesus but finds herself distracted, maybe out of fear or pride or envy or anger. She is listening to some other voice beside his.

Martha is certain that after exchanging a few pleasantries with Jesus, Mary will come help her with all the cooking and the cleaning. But Mary doesn't come. No wonder there was conflict—Martha is trying to get rid of the dust, and Mary is wallowing in it!

So Martha's work undergoes what might be called the "amplification phenomenon." We all know how this works.

Suppose you are emptying the dishwasher. Your spouse or roommate is sitting on the sofa, reading the newspaper, watching television, doing nothing. At first you don't mind—you're sure that when they see how busy you are, they'll join you.

But they don't. You start to get angry. As you get angrier, you bang the plates on the counter with a little more authority. You slam cupboard doors shut so that the sound is clearly audible over the sound of the television set—whose volume keeps getting turned up in an attempt to drown out the clattering crockery.

You want the other person to recognize their slothful selfishness; feel their guilt, fall at your feet, and learn from your work ethic. If that other person has a high guilt tolerance threshold, you have a very loud house.

Martha is rattling the crockery around pretty freely by now. Nothing happens. Mary just keeps sitting there.

You know what is going on in Martha's mind: *The master's here—the guy who teaches about serving all the time—and who's serving? I get so sick and tired of always being the one who does all the work. Pharaoh freed the slaves all right—all but one. Helloo! Mary—clue phone—it's for you.*

That's not all that troubles Martha. Mary is doing something no woman is supposed to do. No other rabbi has a woman disciple. *What will people think? What will happen to Mary's reputation? Jesus' reputation? My reputation? Who will ever marry either one of us if word of this gets around—and it will! Doesn't Mary know a woman's place is in the kitchen?*

Finally Martha can't take it any more. She is certain she is in the right, so she doesn't go to Mary directly. She doesn't even refer to Mary by name. "Lord, don't you care that my sister has left me to do all the work myself? Tell her to help me."

Martha is not criticizing only Mary here. She is not terribly happy with Jesus either. She is putting on the pressure: "If you're compassionate, you'll make certain other people around here do what I want them to do."

Jesus replies, "Martha, Martha...."

"ONE THING IS NEEDED"

When Jesus says your name twice, watch out! Often he calls someone's name when he is especially trying to get their attention:

"Simon, Simon, Satan has asked to sift you as wheat. But I have prayed for you...."

"Saul, Saul, why do you persecute me?"

We sometimes do the same thing. The single most repeated line from an old television show called *The Brady Bunch* featured a frustrated sister, named Jan, who was always complaining about her sibling: "Marsha, Marsha, Marsha...."

"Martha, Martha, Martha...."

I imagine that Jesus says her name with some affection, but goes on to diagnose her condition with surgical precision. What keeps someone from his presence is not just busyness—not just having a lot of things to do. It's distraction.

Jesus puts it this way: "Only one thing is needed." That one thing is the decision to live so continually in Jesus' presence as to be always covered with the dust of the rabbi.

> *The one thing needed is the decision to live so continually in Jesus' presence as to be always covered with the dust of the rabbi.*

Sometimes "sitting at Jesus feet" means we have to stop doing what we have been doing and start doing something else. Maybe we have been driving ourselves to the point of exhaustion, and sitting at Jesus' feet means we have to trust him enough to get some sleep. Maybe we have been watching television while our spouse washes the dishes, and at that moment the dust of the rabbi is all in the kitchen. However, as a general rule we don't need to switch activities in order to be with Jesus. All we need to do is invite him into whatever we are doing at the moment.

Martha got distracted from sitting at Jesus feet. Notice that she wasn't doing bad things. She wasn't breaking the Ten Commandments or gossiping about her neighbors or spending hours lying on the couch watching the Home Shopping Network and ordering stuff with somebody else's credit card. Martha wasn't sinning. She was doing constructive work. She simply wasn't being with Jesus.

"DISTRACTED, WORRIED, UPSET"

The words that describe Martha are, I believe, also the words that describe the great obstacle that keeps many of us from being covered with the dust of the rabbi amid the press of daily activities. Martha is, after all, a follower of Jesus. This isn't Herod or Pontius Pilate or Judas. Martha invited Jesus into her home.

But Martha is distracted from noticing and basking in his presence, and therefore she becomes worried and upset by many things. Not defiant. Not hate-filled. Not rebellious. Just distracted, worried, upset. Same house, different rooms.

Jesus says, "Mary has chosen what is better."

There is a little play on words here. "Better" can be understood to mean "better portion," as in a portion of food. Jesus is saying in effect, "The truth is, Martha, the real banquet going on here is the one I want to serve to you. Mary has chosen the best dish of all. What kind of host would I be if I grabbed the dish out from under her in the middle of the meal? I would never do that. I don't think you really want me to. So come to the table."

THE ART OF LETTING GO

So what is it that keeps us from sitting at Jesus' feet, from being covered with the dust of the rabbi? What keeps us from living in the presence of God? Ironically, it is usually not that we have deliberately chosen to keep him at arm's length. It is something much more insidious and subtle.

I suspect that many of us are like Martha. We have good intentions. We have invited Jesus into our homes. But we end up missing out on his presence—not because we've rejected him, but because we just get overwhelmed by preparations for life. We get distracted. We forget to look for Waldo on the page. Same house, different rooms. And the primary indicator is worry.

Sometimes in our Martha moments we live under the illusion that worry enhances our ability to control the world. Somehow we fear that if we stop worrying about something completely, it will really go wrong. So we worry as if we're still in control of something that's actually completely out of our hands.

Do you ever go bowling? Do you watch what people do after they let go of the ball? They wave at it, talk to it, threaten it. They contort their bodies—they lean to one side, hop on one foot, hunch their shoulders. They act as if they had some kind of magic control over an object that is no longer in their hands.

They have not learned the art of letting go.

When I bowl, certain things are up to me: I can try to get my footwork right, I can bend my knees appropriately, I can handle my backswing with care, I can aim for the right release point. But once I've come to the line and the ball is headed down the alley, I've done all that I can do.

Letting go is not passivity. It is not the same thing as simply resigning oneself to whatever circumstances come along.

So I'll tell you the secret for more joy-filled bowling: When you let it go—let it go.

Letting go is not passivity. To let go is not the same thing as simply resigning oneself to whatever circumstances come along.

I took my daughters to see the movie *Snow White* when they were quite young. I realized partway through the movie—this is a horrible model for them.

Here's a woman who—

—Hides from her stepmother because she feels worried and upset;

—Takes a job doing menial labor for seven short, cranky guys because she thinks she could never find more fulfilling work;

—Sits around passively waiting to get rescued, singing, "Some day my prince will come...."

I wanted my little girls to know that if you're ever in that situation—

—Confront your stepmother face-to-face. Tell her to come to grips with the aging process and you have no intention of being the fall guy because of her neurotic insecurities about fading sexual attractiveness, so it's time for her to find a good therapist.

> The great danger of my worries is that they keep me upset in the kitchen instead of sitting at the feet of the One who loves me.

—Tell the seven short guys to get a life. If they can't handle basic challenges of personal hygiene and housekeeping, they'll have to find some other codependent to enable their domestic passivity.

—Stop waiting for some prince to come around and rescue you. Build deep relationships, find meaningful work, serve the poor, deepen your mind.

And when it is time to choose a prince—let daddy decide who the prince should be.

"Sitting at Jesus' feet" does not mean passively waiting. Often Jesus' desire for us is that we will be active, choosing, risking, stretching, and doing. But it does mean recognizing that he is present here and now, and we don't have to pretend we control the universe any more.

I get "worried and upset" sometimes.

—I have three teenage kids driving now. What if one of them gets in an accident?

—I have a project at work where I don't know what the outcome will be. What if it's not done well?

— There's a confrontation I know I need to have with another person. What if I say the wrong thing? What if they respond badly?

At such times I am tempted to carry the weight of that concern with me all day. And the great danger of those worries is not just that they make my life emotionally unpleasant. It is that they distract me from the presence of God in my life. They keep me upset in the kitchen instead of sitting at the feet of the One who loves me.

If I find I've been worrying about it, I don't beat myself up. And I don't say, "I'll try harder to not worry." The single most powerful step I can take to combat worry is not to try really hard to stop worrying. It is to seek to be covered with the dust of my rabbi.

Then I can allow worry to be a little reminder to have another D.T.R., a kind of prickly invitation to sit at Jesus' feet. I remember that Waldo's on this page too. And I ask for a little more dust.

D.T.R. ON A PLANE

Recently I had to fly to Edmonton, Canada, to speak at a conference. There was no direct flight from San Francisco, so I took a connecting flight through Calgary and had very little time between connections.

We were in the descent into Calgary—you could see trees, cars, people on the ground—when suddenly the plane lurched back upward.

The pilot's voice came on: —"Bad weather rolled in. We couldn't land. We will have to divert the flight and land in another city."

My immediate thought was "God—what's going on? I'm not going to have time to go to another city and still make my flights. I'll miss the conference."

Soon the pilot spoke again—and said the city we were diverting to was Edmonton.

My immediate thought was "God—way to go! Now I don't even have to go to Calgary. This is great!"

We landed at Edmonton. The pilot's voice came back on: "We're just going to land here and refuel, then wait and fly back to Calgary.

No one is allowed to get off the plane. We'll have to sit on the tarmac till the weather clears in Edmonton; they're telling us that will be about three hours."

My immediate thought was "God—what's going on?" This is a new genre of frustration: I'm sitting on the tarmac, looking out at the city where I'm supposed to speak, and I can't get off the plane.

I talked to the flight attendants, to the pilots, to all the passengers in my section. I was told that deboarding would be a violation of international law. I called my church to see if we have any people in international law.

Meanwhile, a whole planeful of passengers was stuck on the ground in Edmonton. A flight crew has only one option for trying to keep people happy: it was open bar time. After an hour or two, I was the only one who really wanted to get off the plane. The passengers around me said, "Tell us your talk. We'd be glad to listen."

There was nothing more I could do. I did, however, remember a line from a book by Dallas Willard that I had read just recently: "At the beginning of each morning I commit my day to the Lord's care.... I have already placed God in charge. I no longer have to manage the weather, airplanes, and other people."

Those were precisely the three elements I could not control. So I let go. Not that it's spiritual to be passive. Rather, I had done all I could think of to do.

A little while later, the pilot told us we could go to a gate and stay in a holding area, but no one could leave. However, it turned out the official in that area had a daughter who was planning to attend the conference I was speaking at. He heard about my situation from the pilot, called someone from Immigration, and had them process me, all by myself, through customs.

A cab ride later, no one was more amazed than I to find me on the platform at Edmonton. And covered with the dust of my rabbi.

GROWING NO FASTER "THAN GRACE ALLOWS"

Part of life we may spend, as Mary did, in the living room during times of quiet and peace. But much of life will be spent "in the kitchen with Martha" — in our place of work. Your kitchen may be an office or a cubicle or a factory floor or a desk at school or a home where you watch over little children or a center where you volunteer. "The kitchen" is generally the place in our society where we are worried and upset over many things. But what if we decided to sit at Jesus' feet even there?

In the next chapter we will think about what an ordinary day might look like if you walked through it covered with the dust of your rabbi. For now, the invitation is to make the D.T.R. prayer the continual, foundational prayer of your spiritual life.

Jesus will come into the kitchen — if we ask him. Many centuries after Martha, another one of Jesus' followers, whom we have already mentioned, spent most of his adult life in the kitchen. Brother Lawrence called himself "the lord of all pots and pans" because he never got higher on the organizational chart than cook and bottle-washer. But he learned how to make his tasks an exercise in sitting at Jesus' feet because he chose the one thing needful. He wrote, "I make it my business only to persevere in his holy presence wherein I keep myself by a simple attention and a general fond regard for God, which I refer to as an actual presence of God."

If you find yourself slow in making progress, take heart. Brother Lawrence writes that for ten years "I was worried that my walk with the Lord wasn't good enough.... Sometimes it got so bad that I thought I was on my way to hell — willfully offending God — and that there was no salvation for me." This was the point, as we saw in the last chapter, when Lawrence stopped expecting to grow any faster. When he accepted his own "slowness," he was at last able to begin to live in grace from one moment to the next. He counseled others to be similarly patient. He writes about one person who was full of good intentions but "wants to go faster than grace allows."

Over time, Lawrence learned to sit at the Lord's feet even while working. "It is not necessary to have great things to do. I turn my little omelets in the pan for the love of God...." In the kitchen, "the lord of all pots and pans" was spattered with more than grease and flour. He was covered with the dust of his rabbi.

CHAPTER 4

THE GREATEST MOMENT OF YOUR LIFE

To see a world in a grain of sand
And a heaven in a wild flower,
Hold infinity in the palm of your hand
And eternity in an hour.

William Blake

If someone were to ask you what was the greatest moment of your life, what would you say? What is the first thing that comes to mind?

I may not know you, but I know that there have been some extraordinary moments in your life: There was the moment you were born—when the clock of your life started ticking and you sucked in your first lungful of breath and the whole adventure started.

There was the moment you took your first step. From that moment on, you were a walker. Your world was never the same. Your mother's world was never the same.

There was the moment you spoke your first word. From that moment on, you a talker. It may be you started talking in that moment and haven't stopped since.

There was the moment you learned how to read a book and a new world opened up to you.

There was the moment you got your first job, made your first friend, went on your first date, experienced your first kiss. I went to a religious college that had firm guidelines about sexual behavior. I used to pray that Jesus would not come back before my wedding night, because I knew it would be the greatest time of my life. (And actually, it *was* pretty good.)

You may remember the moment you fell in love, the moment your child was born, the moment God became real to you, or the moment you discovered how he had gifted you.

But I want to offer another candidate.

I believe that the greatest moment of your life is this moment right here. This tick of the clock. This beat of your heart.

The greatest moment of your life is now.

Not because it's pleasant or happy or easy, but because this moment is the only moment you've got. Every past moment is irretrievably gone. It's never coming back. If you live there, you lose your life.

And the future is always out there somewhere. You can spend an eternity waiting for tomorrow, or worrying about tomorrow. If you live there, you likewise will lose your life.

This moment is God's irreplaceable gift to you. Most of all, this is the moment that matters because this moment is where God is. If you are going to be with God at all, you must be with him *now* — in this moment.

That is why the psalmist says, *"This* is the day the LORD has made; let us rejoice and be glad *in it."*

That is why the prophet says God's mercies never fail because "they are new every morning."

That is why the apostle Paul says, "Be very careful, then, how you live — not as unwise but as wise, making the most of every opportunity."

THE SACRAMENT OF THE PRESENT MOMENT

I believe this can be the greatest moment of your life because this moment is the place where you can meet God. In fact, this moment is the *only* place where you can meet God.

This is why one of the greatest books of spiritual advice ever written was given the inspired title *The Sacrament of the Present Moment.*

A sacrament, according to church tradition, is a "means of grace." It is an ordinary object—the water used in baptism, the cup of communion—that somehow becomes the vessel of the extraordinary, of the divine.

The writer of that book, a spiritual director named Jean Pierre de Caussade, says that each moment of our lives can be a sacrament, a vehicle for God's love and power. "The present moment holds infinite riches beyond your wildest dreams, but you will only enjoy them to the extent of your faith and love.... To discover God in the smallest and most ordinary things, as well as in the greatest, is to possess a rare and sublime faith."

This can be the greatest moment of your life because this moment is the place where you can meet God.

In the same way that every lungful of air gives life to our body, every moment in time can—if we learn to let it—give life to our soul. *This moment* is as God-filled as any we have ever lived. Where's Waldo? He's right here, right now.

Frederick Buechner writes, "Morning, afternoon, evening—the hours of the day, of any day, of your day and my day. The alphabet of grace. If there is a God who speaks anywhere, surely he speaks here: through waking up and working, through going away and coming back again, through people you meet and books you read, through falling asleep in the dark."

THE GREATEST DANGER

If this is the greatest moment of life, I want to suggest what might be the single most dangerous word in the English language. It is found in a story out of the book of Exodus.

The Israelites have been living in slavery for centuries. They want freedom. It's one of the great labor-management conflicts of all time. The labor union (that would be Israel) has a very bad contract, which could be pretty much summarized as "work, then die." Moses is the top union guy, but he doesn't have much leverage, and the rank-and-file are a little shaky.

Management is represented by Pharaoh, and he is a hard-line negotiator.

So God gives Moses some very powerful bargaining chips, known as the ten plagues, to even the playing field. The second plague is one of the most memorable: God sends an army of frogs. "The Nile will teem with frogs. They will come up into your palace and your bedroom and onto your bed,... and into your ovens and kneading troughs."

Old Testament scholars note that the writer is deliberately painting a comic picture to ridicule pretensions of Pharaoh. Frogs in your house; frogs in your *bedroom;* frogs in your *bed*—this is getting seriously disruptive. It is very difficult to get a good night's sleep or enjoy the royal harem with a bed full of frogs. Frogs in the kitchen, on the royal salad, in the royal cereal; frogs in the garage, crunching under wheels of the royal chariot. I would be very careful before using the royal bathroom.

The frogs are out of control. Ken Davis puts it like this:

> Pharaoh can't even back his chariot out of the garage without killing a hundred frogs. His pizza is covered with frogs. If his home is anything like mine, his wife and oldest daughter have been standing on chairs screaming ever since the plague began. His youngest daughter has run out of jars in which to collect and accidentally suffocate them. Frogs are everywhere.

(And guess what Pharaoh's magicians do to show their power? Make more frogs!)

By now Moses has Pharaoh's attention. Pharaoh asks Moses to say a frog-removal prayer. Moses replies with exaggerated courtesy, "I leave to you the honor of setting the time for me to pray ... that you and your houses may be rid of the frogs." And Pharaoh answers in a single word: "Tomorrow."

There's the dangerous word: *tomorrow. Let's wait until tomorrow.*

Anyone reading this story wants to scream at Pharaoh: "What are you thinking?"

Moses says, "You don't have to live with the frogs anymore, Pharaoh. I've got Frog-Be-Gone. Say the word—they're history. Ready?"

And Pharaoh thinks, "Well, but then I'd have to give up my labor force. I'm not ready for that. Maybe if I wait, the frogs will decide to go away by themselves."

Pharaoh has learned—he can live with the frogs. He can tolerate a frog-saturated life. It's not great. There's not much joy in it. But he can survive. He prefers it to the change that would be required by surrendering to Yahweh.

"I'll try another night with the frogs."

MOTIVATED IRRATIONALITY

But Pharaoh isn't the only one who settles for another night with the frogs.

Ken Davis writes about a young woman who came to him for help. She wanted to do God's will, she said, but was confused. She had been in a relationship with a man for six months. He had betrayed her, neglected her, and abused her emotionally and physically. Her question to Ken was "Should I continue seeing him?"

Will you be having frogs with that?

This kind of thing has puzzled the human race a long time. The Greeks had a name for it. Since they were big into *reason*, they couldn't figure out why human beings choose to engage repeatedly in irrational acts that will not just harm others but also destroy themselves. The Greeks called this *akrasia* on the grounds that the gods clouded human thinking and led humans to do crazy things.

More recently, philosopher David Pears has written a book on the same subject: *Motivated Irrationality*.

People persistently tolerate and maintain behavioral patterns that will destroy their own lives:

—A husband holds a grudge against his wife, withholds his love, and nurses his resentment even though he knows it's destroying his own heart, thus making him miserable.

—A sexual addict keeps going back to the Internet even though he knows it's destroying his marriage and self-respect and is eating him up with guilt.

—A man is drowning in debt, being hounded by creditors, and losing his house, then he goes to a financial management seminar and is so impressed by it that he orders $600 worth of material—and puts it on his credit card.

Will you be having frogs with that?

ETERNITY IN DISGUISE

So *tomorrow* may be the most dangerous word in the English language. It may cause us to mismanage finances; it may mean constant problems at work; it can damage relationships; it can eat up our self-esteem and erode our joy. But none of these scenarios gets to the root of the problem.

What matters most is this: God is present in this instant, offering to partner with us in whatever we face. The failure to embrace "the sacrament of the present moment" will keep us from being fully present to God right here, right now.

Not because we consciously say no to God.

We just say, "Tomorrow." Spiritual *akrasia*. Another night with the frogs.

One writer of Scripture puts it like this: "Today, if you hear his voice, do not harden your hearts.... But encourage one another daily, as long as it is called 'today.'"

Tomorrow may be the most dangerous word in the English language.

Most of us have set conditions in our minds, and we think that when those criteria are met, that will be the beginning of great moments. We think the great adventure of partnership with God lies somewhere in the future. We tell ourselves that we will grow closer to God someday when our kids are no longer small and demanding, or when the pressures of work lighten up, or when we become more disciplined, or when our motivation level is higher, or when we just magically grow into spiritual maturity.

Some people go through their whole life in that frame of mind.

"God is closer than you think" means he is available in *this moment right now.* Always now. Only now.

Abraham Heschel writes that other religions often began by setting apart sacred places whereas Israel in the Sabbath set apart a sacred time, for time is the stuff of life.

> For where shall the likeness of God be found? There is no quality that space has in common with the essence of God. There is not freedom enough on the top of a mountain; there is not glory enough in the silence of the sea. *Yet the likeness of God can be found in time, which is eternity in disguise.*

THE DAY STARTS AT NIGHT

Now let's get very concrete. If we want to spend a regular, ordinary day of our life *with Jesus,* what would we actually do? How do we go about trying to receive each moment as a sacrament, a God-charged sliver of grace?

This is what we need to remember at the outset: Spending the day with God does not usually involve doing different things from what we already do. Mostly it involves learning to do what we already do in a new way—*with God.*

Actually, the first task of the day is to go to sleep. In Western culture we think of a day beginning when the sun comes up or when the alarm clock goes off or when Starbucks opens. But the ancient rhythm of days is different. In the creation account, the order is always the same: "And there was evening and there was morning—the first day." Each day in creation begins with evening. In Jewish life, the Sabbath begins not at sunup but at sundown. Eugene Peterson notes that in this way the biblical writers help us to remember: Everything doesn't depend on me. I go to sleep, God goes to work. It's his day. The world keeps spinning, tides ebb and flow, lives begin and end even though I am not there to superintend any of it. God is present when I sleep:

> *In vain you rise early*
> *and stay up late,*

toiling for food to eat—
for he grants sleep to those he loves.

We live in a world where experts tell us we have a sleep debt bigger than the national debt. An estimated 24,000 people die every year in car accidents caused by sleep-deprivation and fatigue. Lack of sleep causes people to argue with spouses and friends, do subpar work, be less loving and more irritable with children and friends, and generally feel miserable. It's hard to live like Jesus if you're sleep deprived. (If you don't believe me, get close to a sleep-deprived person and see.)

But we put up with it. We spend another night with the frogs—whose constant croaking gives us insomnia. We accept feeling tired and sleepy as if it were normal. We complain or even brag about how little we sleep.

People who lead spiritual retreats say the number one barrier for people trying to have a prolonged time of prayer is fatigue. Remember what happened to the disciples in the garden of Gethsemane when Jesus wanted them to pray? They slept. Another time, when they were on the boat in a storm and Jesus was sleeping, they were wide awake with worry and fear. "How can you sleep now?" they pestered him. Their problem was that they slept when they should have been awake, stayed awake when they should have slept. They had a sleep disorder.

Arranging to get enough sleep is actually an act of discipleship.

Arranging to get enough sleep is actually an act of discipleship. Brother Lawrence wrote, "Those who have the wind of the Holy Spirit in the sails glide ahead even while asleep." We will know we are getting enough sleep when we're able to sit comfortably during the day and pray for five minutes or so without nodding off. Avoid coffee, food, or exercise right before bed. Don't watch television late into the night.

Seek to resolve any household conflicts before bedtime. Paul wrote, "Be angry but do not sin; do not let the sun go down on your anger, and do not make room for the devil."

Whatever attitude we habitually go to sleep in becomes normal for us: anger and anxiety, or trust and peace. The way we go to sleep at night sets the tone for how we will live the next day.

Take a few moments to review your day with God. Confess any sin that comes to mind, and ask forgiveness. Where you were blessed today, take time to savor it and say thanks. Give God the last word of the day.

WAKING

How do you wake up *with God*? This may be very hard for you. There are two kinds of people: those who love to get up in the morning, and those who hate those who love to get up in the morning. You may be in the second camp. Maybe you think even Jesus doesn't want to be around you first thing in the morning.

Sometimes people who are not "morning people" put pressure on themselves to have extended times reading Scripture or praying first thing in the morning. If this is effective for you, great. If it is not, you need to memorize these words from a modern-day master of practicing the presence of God. Frank Laubach wrote, "If your devotional life is sleepy and tired—God is probably as tired of it as you are."

Instead of forcing yourself in the morning, try to arrange—as early as you can after you wake up—to have just a few minutes alone with God. Do three things:

1. Acknowledge your dependence on God. *I won't live through this day banking on my own strength and power.*
2. Tell God about your concerns for the day, and ask him to identify and remove any fear in you. I often do this with my calendar for the day open before me.
3. Renew your invitation for God to spend the day with you.

As the psalmist wrote, "In the morning I lay my requests before you and wait in expectation."

Review the foundational truths given at the end of chapter 1, and enter each new day with great confidence. Dietrich Bonhoeffer wrote,

For Christians, the beginning of the day should not be burdened and haunted by the various kinds of concerns they face during the working day. The Lord stands above the new day, for God has made it ... all restlessness, all impurity, all worry and anxiety flee before him.

Therefore, in the early morning hours of the day may our many thoughts and our many idle words be silent, and may the first thought and the first word belong to the one to whom our whole life belongs.

GETTING READY

Something as mundane as washing up in the morning is something we can do with God. In ancient times, cleansing and purification were a very important and highly symbolic part of life. Priests had to go through a very elaborate process of cleansing before entering the temple. This served as a kind of reminder of the need for our souls to be cleansed. The act of baptism developed from the physical act of being washed by water. David asked God, "Cleanse me with hyssop, and I will be clean; wash me, and I will be whiter than snow."

So tomorrow morning, when you are washing your face or taking a shower, make it a moment of prayer: "God, just as this soap and water are cleaning my body, may your Word and your Spirit cleanse my mind and heart. Any impurities — whether wrong intentions, destructive desires, thoughts that lead me away from love and joy and courage — cleanse them entirely."

Let yourself be still for a few moments and see if anything comes to mind. This "letting yourself be still" is a very important part of practicing God's presence. It means you really are allowing him to speak to you.

Then take a moment to remember you have been cleansed by God. Your sins have been washed away forever. Again, this does not require some act of spiritual heroism. You have to wash up anyway. Why not do it with God?

EATING

Food, too, is a gift from God. Jesus told his followers to pray for their daily bread. To the writers of Scripture, food is concrete evidence that God is present and providing. God brings forth "food from the earth,... and bread to strengthen the human heart."

We are actually *commanded* to experience pleasure in food. "Eat your bread with joy," says the writer of Ecclesiastes (who apparently was not on the low-carb South Beach diet).

Make mealtimes an exercise in gratitude. Stop and notice your food. Remember God's goodness to you, and thank him.

Throughout human history, eating with others has been an important act of fellowship and community. Jesus got into a lot of trouble just because of those with whom he ate. In our day that custom of eating in community is being lost.

Robert Putnam writes in his book *Bowling Alone* that the past two decades have witnessed a dramatic change in one traditionally important form of family connectedness—the evening meal. Families eat together much less often, and when they do, there's a good chance they do it in front of a television set. College food services have had to change their formats. Students used to eat an entire meal sitting at the table; now they

In our day the custom of eating in community and fellowship is being lost.

"graze." The colleges serve a generation of people who are not used to sitting at a table for a family meal. If you are part of a family, maybe its time to declare some values and rearrange some priorities.

(If you think trying to turn eating into a spiritual experience is a little far-fetched, consider that for the ancient Hebrews, the other end of the digestive process was a gift of God as well. They actually had a prayer to be said after going to the bathroom: "Blessed art Thou, O God, who hast made the openings in my body.")

Jesus also said that we do "not live on bread alone, but on every word that comes from the mouth of God." As our bodies are fed by food, so our spirits are fed by words with ideas and images. We are flooded by words that can mislead us, so we need to feed our minds each day from the Word of God.

I often feed my mind by taking a thought from Scripture:

—Nothing can separate us from the love of God.

—I can do all things through Christ, who strengthens me.

—God is light, and in him is no darkness at all.

Try to let your mind feast on the Word of God throughout the day.

WORKING

Because we invest so much of our time and identity in our work (whether through a paid job, volunteering, going to school, or working at home), it is perhaps the single most important activity to learn to do together with Jesus.

As Jesus' friends, we start our work day by inviting him to be present with us. I generally start work by sitting at my desk, reviewing my meetings and tasks for the day, and—instead of just worrying about them—asking God if we can partner together in them.

It can be helpful to keep certain physical reminders of God's presence nearby. I have some stones with certain words inscribed on them that speak deeply to me about God's care. One stone reads "Joy." Another says "Courage." A third one just has the word "Yes." Each reminds me of the spirit in which I want to work. They tell me that I'm not alone. Also, I have a crown of thorns and a nail on a credenza that speaks to me of God's sacrificial love. I have pictures of the people I love, through whom God most often speaks to me.

Every few hours I try to remember to take a break. That may be something as simple as sitting up straight and taking a few deep breaths; as I breathe, I remember that I am being filled with God's Spirit. I may look out the window at something growing outside, or listen to music that speaks to my soul. I try to remember to look for Waldo.

When I get evaluations and feedback at work, I try to listen for God's voice in it. Often he speaks to me through the comments of others—which is good, because we tend to get more feedback about our lifestyle at work than in almost any other arena.

At the end of my workday I used to become discouraged at what I didn't accomplish. Now I try to do what God did during the week of creation: to look at what has been accomplished that day and celebrate what is good. I thank God that he has partnered with me through the day. I take a moment to ask him to partner with me tomorrow.

You have to go to work anyway. Why not do it with Jesus?

INTERRUPTIONS

Some moments each day involve interruptions from unexpected tasks or demands. How do we deal with interruptions? Dietrich Bonhoeffer offers some good counsel.

> We must be ready to allow ourselves to be interrupted by God. God will constantly be crossing our paths and canceling our plans by sending us people with claims and requests. We may pass them by, preoccupied with our more important tasks, like the priest who passed by the man who had fallen among thieves.

> When we do that, we by-pass the visible sign of the cross raised on our path to show us that, not our way, but God's way must be done.

It is possible that when the phone rings or there's a knock on the door or somebody wants a favor or I see a person with a flat tire on the side of the road, it is a divine appointment. God has come close.

Standing in line—which always feels like an interruption to my schedule—no longer has to be an exercise in frustration for me. It can become (and sometimes does—not always, but sometimes) a moment when I look at my fellow standers and talk to God about them and say silent prayers of blessing for them. For some of them, that may be the only prayer they receive all day.

This doesn't mean that anytime I'm interrupted I have to do what the interrupter wants. It doesn't mean that attention deficit disorder is actually a form of deep spirituality.

It is possible that what we see as an inconvenient interruption is a divine appointment.

But I wonder: What would Jesus' ministry have looked like if he had never allowed himself to be interrupted? Many of his greatest miracles and most unforgettable encounters were Spirit-prompted interruptions.

Once on his way into town Jesus was interrupted by a blind man named Bartimaeus, and he restored his sight. Another time, he was on his way to do one good deed when a woman suffering from chronic illness touched him, causing the power to go out of him, and he healed her. He was interrupted by a leper and touched and healed him. He was eating a meal at a Pharisee's house when a sinful woman crashed the party, weeping a pool of tears at his feet, and he forgave her. He was interrupted right up to his hanging on the cross—which looked like the ultimate interruption of his ministry, but was in fact the greatest work his Father had for him to do.

ODDS AND ENDS

Then there are all the moments that don't fit into any particular category. Think of paying bills and running errands and greeting those you live with when you come home from work. All these can become moments of companionship. For instance, what would it look like if, while you were driving, you were to drive *with Jesus*? Would you have to drive any slower than you normally do? If you could see Jesus with you in the car, would he have a worried look on his face and feel the need to fasten a seat belt? Would you need to start talking to other drivers differently than you do?

Maybe you are a newspaper reader. Some people feel guilty about spending too much time reading the paper in the morning and not enough time reading the Bible. But—at least for today—instead of trying to do a heroic amount of Bible reading, go ahead and read the newspaper. Just read it with Jesus. Talk to him about what you read. When it raises a concern in you, ask him to help the people you're reading about.

Maybe you are a TV-watcher. Many of us feel vaguely guilty about watching too much television, and we may handle this by pretending God doesn't exist while we're watching. Kind of like a five-year-old who closes his eyes when he goes to the forbidden cookie jar under the theory that if he can't see anything, his parents can't either. Go ahead and watch, only today—watch it with Jesus. If you are enjoying it, tell him. And if you wonder whether you're watching too much or watching the wrong things, trust that he will speak to you about this.

Pick an ordinary day when you will actually try this "with-God" experiment. Don't attempt to do a lot of new heroic things. Just do the things you normally do. Only do them with God. Because if you can spend one ordinary day with Jesus, you can spend every day with him. One day at a time.

In our culture we often talk about embracing the moment and seizing the day. Although these ideas express a deep longing in our hearts, they are somehow not powerful enough to transform us. I think this is because we were not meant to embrace moments, because moments and days, like the pages of a newspaper, can be filled with bad news as well as good.

We are not meant to embrace moments, but to embrace God. Moments are not always good; God is never anything else but good. Moments are simply the place where we meet him. Every moment. Starting now.

Or, you could do another night with the frogs.

CHAPTER 5

A BEAUTIFUL MIND

A mystic is anyone who believes that, when you talk to God,
God talks back.

Frank Laubach

He was hailed as one of the most brilliant minds of the twentieth century. The word *genius* gets thrown around pretty loosely; but in his case it was an understatement. His thesis on the dynamics of human conflict would revolutionize economic theory and eventually win the Nobel Prize. He did this work at an age when many people are still trying to figure out how to move away from Mom and Dad. Before he was out of his twenties he was a distinguished professor at MIT.

But at the height of his career John Nash suffered a breakdown. He interrupted a lecture to announce he was on the cover of *Life* magazine disguised as the pope. He claimed foreign governments were communicating with him through the media, and he turned down a prestigious post at the University of Chicago because, he said, he was about to be named Emperor of Antarctica.

In the movie *A Beautiful Mind,* based on a book with the same title, we see the characters and hear the voices that exist only in his head, unconnected to reality. They made him feel important—as if he were the center of the universe. They played on his darkest fears. When he listened to them, they destroyed his relationships, distorted his perceptions, made him obsessive, irrational, and terrified. They led to death.

Paranoid delusion is one of the most difficult forms to treat in all of psychopathology. When I was finishing my doctorate in clinical psychology, I worked for a time with a client who suffered from full-blown paranoia. He was convinced that the FBI had wiretapped his home, that his neighbors were spying on him, that strange voices were speaking directly to him through his televison set. The most difficult feature of his condition was that the voices seemed absolutely real to him. To tell him they were not real would be like asking you or me to distrust the existence of our boss or best friend. He eventually grew better, thanks largely to a form of medication that was not available in the early days of John Nash's illness.

Which is what makes the story of John Nash so remarkable. He was actually able to learn, over time, the art of discernment. He learned to test the voices, to find out which ones were false and which ones were true.

He had to learn to not listen to the ones that lead to death. He learned not to dwell on what they said. He learned not to do what they requested. And while never completely freed from his illness, he discovered that over time their hold on his mind could be greatly weakened. He experienced, in a sense, a revolution of the mind.

Nash speaks at one point in the film about how in a way his battle is the battle of all of us. "I'm not so different from you," he says to his friend. "We all hear voices. We just have to decide which ones we are going to listen to."

"WE ALL HEAR VOICES"

Two people suffer from cancer. One becomes bitter and despairing while the other is a beacon of honesty and hope to the people around them. Their cancer is the same. The difference is in their minds.

Two people live with meager financial resources. One of them is consumed by envy and discontent; the other is radiant with gratitude and servanthood. Their net worth is the same. The difference is in their minds.

Two people reach the top of their organizations. One uses power for self-aggrandizement and control; the other uses it to enhance the lives of everyone in the community. Their titles are the same. The difference is in their minds.

Two people live in a universe where God is always present. One of them decides that "in all my thoughts there is no room for God." The other says, "Always before me I set you, O Lord." God's offer of availability is the same. The difference is in their minds.

The mind is an instrument of staggering potential. But its potential is not measured by IQ or academic degrees. For it is in our minds that we live in conscious awareness of and interaction with God.

"We all hear voices...." At least I do. Some of them are distorted and destructive; they speak to me thoughts of envy and resentment and fear. Some of them are healthy and strong; they speak words of love and truth. The ones I listen to shape my life.

But there's one Voice above all to which we're called to listen. Jesus said that he is the Good Shepherd and that "his sheep follow him because they know his voice. But they will never follow a stranger; in fact, they will run away from him because they do not recognize a stranger's voice."

Throughout history, those who have practiced God's presence most have insisted that they hear his voice. They have learned, so to speak, to program their minds to be constantly receiving the divine channel. "The word is very near you; it is in your mouth and in your heart so you may obey it."

Social reformer Dorothy Day, who did much work on behalf of the poor in the twentieth century, spoke of what she called her "notions" — ideas that had the unmistakable stamp of God's authorship in her mind. George Fox and the Quaker tradition called them "concerns." Others speak of "promptings" or "leadings." Thomas Kelly wrote of "divine breathings."

> *The mind is an instrument of staggering potential, but its potential is not measured by IQ or academic degrees.*

Now it is our turn. In this chapter we look at how to cultivate the kind of mind that is receptive to God's presence and voice. If we are ever to experience the closeness of God, it means a revolution of the mind. How do I make my mind the kind of place where God dwells?

I MUST BELIEVE THAT GOD REALLY WILL SPEAK TO ME

If we are going to be in a personal relationship with someone, there must be some two-way communication. Even the most uncommunicative husband has to grunt every once in a while or it isn't a marriage—it's a monologue. The God of the Bible is not limited to grunting.

So being *with* God is something that takes place primarily in our thoughts, our mind. Even at the purely human level, being *with* someone is never purely physical. Two people may occupy space in the same room, but if one of them is sleeping or in a coma—or perhaps engrossed in watching a football game—they are not really *with* each other. (If you have ever had a relationship with someone who worships at the cult of the Remote Control, you know the difference between "being in the same room as" and "being *with*.") Being with another person requires what might be called *interactive awareness*. I am aware that you are with me, and the things that you do and say are influencing the stream of thoughts and feelings going on inside me. We interact.

Because we are finite beings, we use our bodies in the process of being with. Because we are finite, we do not have "direct access" to each other's thoughts. You make audible sounds or touch my skin or gesture with your hands, and in so doing you influence or guide my thoughts.

But God is infinite rather than finite, so he is able to guide our thoughts directly. He can speak to us through Scripture, of course, or through the words of another person. But he also has "direct access," so to speak; he can plant a thought directly in our minds. Anytime. Anywhere. In one sense, his communication is the same as that of our friend or roommate, with the one great exception that he doesn't need any mediating sights or sounds. In other words, it is possible that any given thought that runs through our minds might have been guided there by God—and we may not even know it.

This means that if we are to meet God at all, the *place* where we dwell with him will be in our minds. Thoughts happen. And some of those thoughts come from God.

I RECOGNIZE THAT I CANNOT CONTROL HIS SPEAKING

There is much about God's speaking that is mystery to me. One thing I know for sure: There are no formulas. I cannot control God's communicating with me. I cannot force him to speak through my piety, sincerity, or hard work. The wind blows where it will, Jesus once said.

One morning I was in my office at my former church and was sweating bullets over a midweek message that refused to be born, or even conceived. This is a pain, any male preacher will tell you, compared to which having a physical baby is a walk in the park. (Women preachers who may have had an actual baby also know this.) Bill Hybels, the senior pastor, bounced into my office with the happy report that his message for that weekend was already finished. Meanwhile, I had nothing. A little later on, he came back in to tell me that he had a brainstorm for his message the following week, and that was done too. He was beaming. I was so happy for him.

Before the end of the day, Bill stopped by to say that he had a talk to give overseas in a few weeks, and he had a terrific idea for that one as well. And I realized what was going on.

God was giving Bill *my* messages.

I cannot force God to give me the guidance or help I think I need. There may be a good reason for his remaining silent sometimes. (At the human level, wise parents and good friends often recognize the need for silence, so surely at the divine level, God does as well.) For instance, I have never received clear guidance at any major vocational crossroads of my life. When I was finishing grad school, when I was going to my first church, when I was contemplating marriage, and even not that long ago when I began to think about leaving Chicago to come to Menlo Park—I would tell God that if he'd just send me a postcard with directions, I would gladly obey. But the postcard never came.

This used to frustrate me, but I have come to suspect there is a good reason for it. God knows me well enough to know that if I have to grapple with these decisions—to think and struggle and examine my motives and assess the future and have conversations with wise friends and take responsibility for choices—I will grow in ways that would never be possible if I simply received a postcard in the mail. And God's primary concern for me is not my external situation—it's the kind of person I'm becoming. *God's silence does not mean his absence.* He is surely capable of making himself understood when he has direction to give.

I cannot force God to give me the guidance or help I think I need. There may be a good reason for his remaining silent sometimes.

So we cannot force God's speaking, and it is not wise to try. But there are things we can do to make our minds increasingly receptive to his presence in our thoughts.

Every thought holds the promise of carrying me into God's presence.

In the painting on the ceiling of the Sistine Chapel, God and the man he created are just a hairbreadth apart. How far apart is that? Closer than you think. *God is never more than a single thought away.* Even if I haven't thought of him for days. Even when I have been immersed in selfishness and sin.

Let's look at an example of the power of our thoughts to pull us toward or away from God. Cognitive psychologists say every thought carries a little "emotional charge," pulling us toward or away from some emotion like anger or joy. In one experiment, subjects who completed the sentence "I'm glad I'm not a ..." five times ended up feeling more happy than when they started. On the other hand, subjects who completed the sentence "I wish I were a ..." the same number of times ended up feeling worse.

In a similar way, I think that all our thoughts carry with them a kind of spiritual charge. Paul says in his letter to the church at Rome that when the Holy Spirit is present and at work in a human mind, he always moves it in the direction of life: "The mind controlled by the Spirit is life and peace." On the other hand, the mind that shuts itself off to the presence of God tends toward destructiveness: "The mind controlled by the sinful nature is death."

We might think about it this way: There is a ceaseless stream of thoughts running through your mind at lightning speed. Picture each thought as a bead strung across a wire.

You read this book and think about a sentence, then you go to turn a page and notice you've been chewing on your nails, which reminds you of your anxiety about your boss, which prompts a little anger fantasy about what you'd *really* like to say to him, at which point your mind turns back to this book.

This is your mind. You are having a series of thoughts. Sometimes your mind seems slow and feels like this:

Sometimes a whole day goes by, and it feels as if your entire brain activity looked like this:

The reality is that your mind is never still. You are having thoughts, observations, perceptions, and ideas at such a staggering rate that you don't even remember the vast majority of them.

In reality, each thought we have carries with it a little spiritual power, a tug toward or away from God. No thought is purely neutral.

Every thought is either enabling and strengthening you to be able to cope with reality to live a kingdom kind of life, or robbing you of that life.

Every thought is — at least to a small extent — God-breathed or God-avoidant; leading to death or leading toward life.

In time, if we listen carefully, we can learn to recognize his voice. Not infallibly, of course. But the kind of thoughts that come from God are those in line with the fruit of the Spirit; they move us toward love and joy and peace and patience. And we will learn that there are other thoughts that are *not* likely to be God speaking. For instance, nowhere in the Bible does it say, "And then God worried." So I can be quite confident that thoughts that move me toward a paralyzed anxiety are not from God.

SAYING "YES" WHEN HE SPEAKS

What does it look like when God "guides our thoughts"? On a recent flight, I was sitting in an aisle seat (my preference) next to a carefully dressed, dignified, white-haired man in his late eighties. Early in the flight he leaned over and said to me as softly as he could, "I hope I don't disturb you too much on this flight. I have a problem with frequent urination."

I thought of how embarrassing it must be for a man to have to give that information to a total stranger on a plane. He went on to explain that his wife was traveling with him, but the airline had placed her in the middle seat of the row in front of us.

A thought quietly entered my mind: *Offer to change seats with her.* Was this thought from God? I can't prove it, of course, but it seemed like the kind of thing that he would say. I made the offer. They accepted it. I know what a small act it was. Someone farther down the road to servanthood than I wouldn't have hesitated at all; they would have just seen it. But God is gracious to communicate to us even at the point of our immaturity in a way that we can understand. John Calvin has a beautiful metaphor for this:

> For who is so devoid of intellect as not to understand that
> God, in so speaking, lisps with us as nurses are wont to do

with little children?... In doing so, he must, of course, stoop far below his proper height.

God stoops. God lisps.

Our job is to be ruthless about saying yes when we believe God is speaking to us. Every time we do, we will get a little more sensitive to hearing him the next time. Our mind becomes a little more receptive, a little more tuned in to God's channel. On the other hand, when we say "no, I'd rather stay in my aisle seat," we make ourselves a little less likely to hear him in the future.

THE "WITHOUT-GOD" MIND

The natural tendency of my mind apart from God is toward death, not life. Psychologist Mihalyi Csikszentmihalyi (pronounced "chick-SENT-me-high") has done years of research in which thousands of subjects are given pagers that go off at random intervals. People have to write down what they are doing and thinking and feeling when that happens. One of the most striking findings of these studies involves the effect of solitude.

Every time we say yes to God we will get a little more sensitive to hearing him the next time.

When people are alone, undistracted by noise or activity, their minds naturally drift toward an awareness of discontentment, a sense of inadequacy, anxiety about the future, and a chronic sense of self-preoccupation. Csikszentmihalyi writes,

> Contrary to what we tend to assume, the normal state of the mind is chaos.... When we are left alone, with no demands on attention, the basic disorder of the mind reveals itself. With nothing to do, it begins to follow random patterns, usually stopping to consider something painful or disturbing.... Entropy is the normal state of consciousness.
>
> To avoid this condition, people are naturally eager to fill their minds with whatever information is readily available, as long as it distracts attention from turning inward and dwelling

on negative feelings. This explains why such a huge proportion of time is invested in watching television, despite the fact that it is very rarely enjoyed.

This is why people generally flee from solitude.

When parents want to punish a child, the number one method is a time-out.

The most hated punishment prison inmates receive is solitary confinement.

Why are these so feared? Because people hate to be alone with their minds.

Television is attractive because it distracts us, but of course in the long run it simply makes our minds that much weaker and more dependent on outside stimulation to keep us entertained.

This is precisely what Paul is getting at when he warns the church at Ephesus not to live any longer like those who are far from God in the "futility of their thinking." They are locked up in death-producing thoughts. The ultimate outcome of such living is described by Paul in his letter to the church at Rome: God "gave them over to a depraved mind."

These are some of the most chilling words in Scripture. Someone given over to a depraved mind experiences unending discontent; relentless fear, and unending self-obsession. A person like this doesn't need any outside form of torture to punish them. This is the depth of human misery and pain, and God just "gives them over" to it.

But God never *desires* that our minds be filled with despair or tormented by unsatisfied longings. God's desire is for us to have a mind permeated by life-giving thoughts.

ONLY GOD CAN CHANGE A MIND

Paul wrote to the church at Rome for people to "be transformed by the renewing of your minds." He doesn't say "transform yourselves by renewing your minds." Only God can change a mind. This explains why Paul wrote to Timothy that God has "not given us the spirit of fear; but of power, and of love, and of a *sound* mind." When God is present in a mind, it begins to flow with a new kind of thought.

But there is a role for us to play. We can, by choice and by our actions, invite God to be present in our mind. Or we can close the door to him. It all depends on what kind of mind we want to cultivate. So let's walk through three options.

1. Maybe your goal is debauchery, lechery, and depravity. It's not hard to cultivate a mind like this. You can do it. Just be careful about what you do and don't put into your mind.

You will find your thoughts running along these lines:

— He's more successful than I am, and that makes me feel bad. I hope he fails at something.

— There's a girl jogging up ahead. I wonder if she's attractive enough so I can get a little jolt of sexual gratification by looking at her.

— That guy has a more expensive car than I do. He must be pretty greedy.

— That guy has a junkier car than me. He must be pretty low on the totem pole.

— What if I don't succeed at school today? I'll carry a cloud of anxiety all day.

— I'm late for this meeting. The truth is, I didn't allow enough time to get here, but I'll just say it's because the traffic was bad. I'll spin the truth to manage people's impressions.

— She's so attractive, I feel threatened by her. I'm going to believe bad things about her.

The moods that will dominate your life are resentment, anxiety, unsatisfied desire. The key to maintaining this inner life is found in Psalm 10:4:

In their pride the wicked do not seek him;
In all their *thoughts* there is no room for God.

It's not hard to cultivate this kind of mind. All you have to do is avoid contact with anything that would disrupt this flow of thoughts. Avoid Scripture, avoid wise and honest people who know you deeply, avoid honest self-examination, avoid contact with people in need who might move you to compassion. Avoid looking for Waldo.

Mostly you have to make sure that in your thoughts there is no room for God. Stay tuned to other channels.

2. If your goal is to have a mediocre spiritual life, you can do a half-and-half deal.

The Bible talks about this. One writer speaks of a condition called "double-mindedness." In the Jewish tradition it is called the *yetzer hara,* the wayward heart. Jesus himself refers to a church suffering from what he called "lukewarmness"; it is neither cold nor at the boiling point. It doesn't experience any change of properties.

This condition enables you to get the worst of all worlds: you experience a kind of chronic, low-level, hidden debauchery so you're frustrated by all the fun you think that major-league debauchery professionals are having. Yet you get just enough spiritual-religious input so you have chronic, low-level guilt about the amount of depravity you *are* maintaining.

How do you pursue this goal?

Get sporadic spiritual input. Go to church sometimes. Read the Bible once in a while—but without clarity about how you want it to shape your mind. Pray sporadically—when you're in trouble. But then mostly fill your mind with the things that everybody else in our culture fills their minds with. Just keep spiritual channel-surfing.

There is a third alternative.

3. Make your mind the dwelling place of God.

The goal here is to have a mind in which the glorious Father of Jesus is always present and gradually crowds out every distorted belief, every destructive feeling, every misguided intention. You will know your mind is increasingly "set on God" when the moods that dominate your inner life are love, joy, and peace—the three primary components of the fruit of the Spirit.

　　—I face a crisis. I remember that I am not alone. "The Lord is my Shepherd" has become part of my mental furniture. I don't have to be bigger or smarter than I am. I live at peace.

—Somebody praises me. My first thought and feelings move toward God's goodness in my life. I experience a little surge of joy.

—Somebody condemns me. I remember that God supports me because he loves me. I don't have to appease or blast the critic. I can love.

—I take my daughter to Krispy Kreme. I'm amazed at how good God is to create such a human being. I'm filled with joy. Joy and Krispy Kremes. Grateful that God thought up Krispy Kreme.

God is never more than a thought away. Frank Laubach wrote,

We can keep two things in mind at once. Indeed, we cannot keep one thing in mind more than half a second. Mind is a flowing something. It oscillates. Concentration is merely the continuous return to the same problem from a million angles. So my problem is this: can I bring God back in my mind-flow every few seconds so that God shall always be in my mind as an after-image, shall always be one of the elements in every concept and precept? I choose to make the rest of my life an experiment in answering this question.

To make my mind a home for Jesus, I deliberately fill my mind with the kinds of things God says are important. Paul puts it like this: "Finally, brothers and sisters, whatever is true, whatever is noble, whatever is right, whatever is pure, whatever is lovely, whatever is admirable—if anything is excellent or praiseworthy—think about such things."

We often want to be able to hear guidance from God about impor-tant decisions such as whom to marry or what job to take. But we also want to reserve the right to feed our minds on whatever junk comes along. Whatever repeatedly enters the mind occupies the mind, even-tually shapes the mind, and will ultimately express itself in what you do and who you become. The events we attend, the material we read (or don't), the music we listen to, the images we watch, the conversa-tions we hold, the daydreams we entertain—these are shaping our minds. And ultimately they make our minds receptive or deaf toward the still small voice of God.

Paul says, "We take *every thought* captive." That sounds exhausting! Do we have to filter 185 billion mental images through the course of our lives? But of course, we don't do this on our own. God will help us fill our minds with the right kind of thoughts. God is never more than a thought away.

> *What we say, do, hear, or imagine ultimately makes our minds receptive or deaf toward the still small voice of God.*

I received a letter recently from someone I barely know, someone who knows me mostly from hearing me speak. He named a flaw of mine — nothing that would be terribly scandalous, but something that's egocentric enough to be embarrassing to me. He admonished me.

When I read his words, it was like a little scalpel going into me. Here is what I would be tempted to think: *This is so humiliating! Somebody sees junk in me. It's old junk that I've wrestled with for years. It's not changing, and it will never change. I wonder how many other people see it whom I don't even know.*

If I think that way, I spiral down into discouragement, paralysis, and self-pity. It's death. Those thoughts need to be filtered out. So when I recognized the downward spiral of those thoughts taking place, I said a little prayer asking for God to help guide my thoughts.

These are the thoughts that ran through my mind: *This is exactly what I needed to hear if I wasn't going to be stuck in something. These words can help me grow. They identify a concrete piece of behavior that can be changed.*

Then came another string of thoughts: *Why should I want people to think I'm better than I am? People who know me know the truth about me anyway.*

I have a friend who — when someone in our circle does something goofy — pretends the phone rings, and he says, "It's the jerk store — they say they're out of you." People who know me know my aisle in the jerk store.

Then comes another thought: *God still loves me anyway. This is precisely what grace is for.*

It's a funny thing: There was still some pain, I was somewhat embarrassed, but part of me was glad. I could grow. (By the way, by this time you have read far enough in this book to pick up any number of flaws to which I'm prone. Don't write. I can only process so much at a time.)

LEANING INTO COMMUNITY

Often God uses other people to help us discern his voice. There are certain people in your life whose words consistently guide you toward truth and joy and love. Be sure you make time for those people.

In a powerful scene toward the end of *A Beautiful Mind*, John Nash comes out of the classroom and encounters a man waiting to speak to him whom he has never seen before.

The man says to Nash, "I've come to talk with you about being awarded the Nobel Prize."

Nash is silent for a moment. He has suffered too much from listening to voices of grandiosity. He is not going to listen to the voice on his own. He stops one of his students: "Excuse me—do you see a man standing here? Is he in your line of vision? Is he for real?"

If we are serious about interactive awareness of God, we will have to spend some time listening for him.

The student says yes, so Nash turns to the man: "Okay. I'll listen to you now."

That is a humbling thing for a man with a brilliant mind to have to do.

Nash learned to lean into community to discern which voices are worth listening to and which are delusional.

We can do that. *The spirit of Jesus speaks through the community of Jesus.* When you are not sure about a voice, go to some trusted friends and discuss it. Is this voice giving a true sense of conviction or neurotic guilt? Is this a calling or just grandiosity? Lean into community.

LEARNING TO LISTEN

Of course, if we are serious about interactive awareness of God, it means we will have to spend some time listening for him. Samuel's prayer to God was, "Speak, LORD, for your servant is listening." All too often my prayer is, "Listen, God, your servant is speaking." Listening can involve a variety of practices: reading, solitude and silence, conversations, watching the beauty of a sunset, listening to great music. Perhaps the oldest and most powerful practice is meditation on Scripture.

We are told in the book of Genesis that Isaac "went out to the field one evening to meditate."

What do you think he was doing out there? The word *meditate* scares a lot of people. It sounds alien to us. "Don't Buddhists meditate?" people wonder. And of course, they do. But as a friend of mine says, they eat breakfast, too, and we don't have a problem with that.

The reality is that everyone meditates. Meditation is simply the process by which the mind dwells with some intensity and duration over a thought or image. We may meditate over *Sports Center*, the Dow Jones average, a *Simpsons* episode on television, or what the scale reading was this morning. The issue when it comes to meditation is *what*, not *if*. The mind observes the impulse to meditate the way the body observes the law of gravity.

Scripture has a lot to say about meditating wisely. The psalmist talks about the fruitful person as one whose "delight is in the law of the LORD, and on his law he meditates day and night." Joshua commanded people to "not let this Book of the Law depart from your mouth; meditate on it *day and night.*"

Meditation is not a confusing activity. In a sense, meditation is just positive worry. If you know how to worry, you know how to meditate.

To practice, take the statement from Psalm 16:8: "I have set the LORD always before me. Because he is at my right hand, I will not be shaken."

Say these words out loud several times, and let them roll around in your mind.

"I have set the LORD always before me...." Take some time to imagine how this might get actually experienced in your life. What would it be like to wake up with God on my mind? What would it feel like at night if I were aware of him as I dropped off to sleep? What would my conversations be like with other people if God were the unseen third party present? What would work or school be like if I were continuously speaking to God as I sat at my desk, asking for his help and guidance, not carrying the burden by myself?

I reflect on the idea that the Lord is "at my right hand." The right hand was assumed in biblical times to be the hand of action, the hand that does the work. Therefore the right hand was the place of honor. (If you are left-handed and don't like that, too bad! The Bible is right-handed.)

Because "I will not be shaken," I picture myself receiving bad news, facing opposition; picturing somebody important who doesn't like me. My work goes badly, but I'm not shaken. I'm living in peace.

As I meditate, these thoughts move from my head to my heart. I begin to think, "I want a life like that."

Then these thoughts move to my will: "God, I choose for my life to be so. I will do whatever is needed to have it so."

And then comes the thought *"I am with you."* Something that simple. And he *is* with me. I'm tuned in to the right channel.

At last I begin to understand that what makes a mind great — what makes a *beautiful mind* — is stored goodness that overflows into a beautiful life.

BEYOND BEING SMART

Jenna works with a choir of kindergarten kids at our church. One member, a little older than the other children, is a boy who has Down syndrome. When the boy first started attending, he would generally observe, but not sing. He liked the rhythm of the music and the energy of other children, but he was mostly a spectator.

Then one day the kids sang a song based on a statement by the apostle Paul: "He who began a good work will not give up on me...." Jenna taught the choir hand motions — pointing toward the sky for

"He who began," crossing their hands like an umpire signaling safe when they sang "will *not* give up," pointing to themselves at the word "me." It wasn't until they had run through the song several times that she looked over at the Down syndrome boy and saw that this time he wasn't just watching. He looked Jenna in the eye as his little finger shot up in the air, and out of the overflow of his heart his little mouth spoke, "He who began a good work will not give up on *me*."

When I was young, I wanted badly to be smart. I didn't like it when other kids in my class got better grades than I did. I wanted to be the one with the answers.

Now I'd like to have a mind that stores up good things. The way that boy does. I'd like a beautiful mind.

CHAPTER 6

WALDO JUNIOR

Loving God and loving one's neighbor are really the same thing.
Brother Lawrence

Christ addresses me in the voice of each person I meet.
Esther de Waal

Isaiah cried out to God one day, "Oh, that you would rend the heavens and come down!" And one day God did.

How could Isaiah have known—how can any of us know—what "coming down" would cost God? The story of incarnation is the story of love.

Father Damien was a priest who became famous for his willingness to serve lepers. He moved to Kalawao, a village on the island of Molokai in Hawaii that had been quarantined to serve as a leper colony. For sixteen years he lived in their midst. He learned to speak their language. He bandaged their wounds, embraced the bodies no one else would touch, preached to hearts that would otherwise have been left alone. He organized schools, bands, and choirs. He built homes so that the lepers could have shelter. He built two thousand coffins by hand so that when they died, they could be buried with dignity. Slowly, it was said, Kalawao became a place to live rather than a place to die, for Father Damien offered hope.

Father Damien was not careful about keeping his distance. He did nothing to separate himself from his people. He dipped his fingers in the *poi* bowl along with the patients. He shared his pipe. He did not always wash his hands after bandaging open sores. He got close. For this the people loved him.

Then one day he stood up and began his sermon with two words: "We lepers...."

Now he wasn't just helping them. Now he was one of them. From this day forward he wasn't just on their island; he was in their skin. First he had chosen to live as they lived; now he would die as they died. Now they were in it together.

One day God came to earth and began his message: "We lepers...." Now he wasn't just helping us. Now he was one of us. Now he was in our skin. Now we were in it together.

The story of incarnation is the story of love. Many people didn't recognize him as God, of course. They were looking for someone a little flashier. They expected more in the way of special effects, not someone who would take on all our limitations. He came as Waldo. Many people saw him, but only a few recognized him. Those who missed him did not generally do so out of a lack of knowledge. What blinded them was pride.

WALDO JUNIOR

When it was time for him to leave the earth, Jesus said that his friends were lucky, because then the Holy Spirit could come and form a new community. Although his bodily presence was leaving the earth, this new community would become Jesus' *new* body—"the body of Christ"—through which his presence would get extended.

Because of this, some writers of Scripture say things about God being present in people that take our breath away when we really think about them:

— "Where two or three are gathered together in my name, *there am I in the midst of them.*"

— "Whatever you did for the least of these brothers of mine, *you did for me.*"

— "Whoever is kind to the poor lends to the Lord."

— "No one has ever seen God; but if we love one another, God lives in us and his love is made complete in us."

When Saul-alias-Paul was busy terrorizing and imprisoning Jesus' followers, he was intercepted by Jesus' asking him, "Why do you persecute *me*?" Of course, Jesus had already ascended to heaven by this time. Saul was persecuting men and women—members of the church. But apparently Jesus identifies so closely with his people that when they suffer, he suffers. What Saul did to the church he was doing to Jesus.

It is even harder to recognize God's presence in the second Waldo than it was in the first one.

Initially Jesus was present on earth through the body that was conceived in Mary's womb. But after the ascension he became present on earth through another Body—the community of his followers. It's as if there were a second incarnation. The church is, in a sense, Waldo Junior.

Of course, it is even harder to recognize God's presence in the second Waldo than it was in the first one. C. S. Lewis writes about this dynamic in his book *The Screwtape Letters*, which takes the form of letters from a master demon (Screwtape) to his nephew (Wormwood) about how to undermine his patient's spiritual growth. Screwtape advises Wormwood to help his patient miss God's presence in people by appealing to his *pride*:

> When he gets to his pew and looks round him he sees just that selection of his neighbors whom he has hitherto avoided. You want to lean pretty heavily on those neighbors. Make his mind flit to and fro between an expression like "the body of Christ" and the actual faces in the next pew. It matters very little, of course, what kind of people that next pew really contains. You may know one of them to be a great warrior on the Enemy's side. No matter. Your patient, thanks to Our Father Below, is a fool. Provided that any of those neighbors sing out of tune, or have boots that squeak, or double chins, or odd

clothes, the patient will quite easily believe that their religion must therefore be somehow ridiculous.

In some way we don't fully understand, God has incarnated himself again. He is present to us through people: a real estate agent, a bank teller, a next-door neighbor, a homeless man. However, most of us don't see. When it comes to people, it is perhaps supremely true: *God is closer than you think.*

THE CASE OF NAAMAN

In Scripture we see that God often mediates his presence and sends his messages through people. He confronted David through the prophet Nathan: "Thou art the man!" He encouraged Esther through her Uncle Mordecai: "Who knows but that you have come to royal position for such a time as this?" He blessed Joseph and Mary through an old man named Simeon. He gave advice to Moses through his father-in-law. (And as my children get closer to marrying age, the idea of God speaking through a father-in-law sounds more and more plausible.)

But one of the classic examples of God speaking repeatedly to someone through people involves a man named Naaman. So let's look at his struggle to hear the message God sent to him through some unlikely people.

Naaman was a military man. He had risen in the ranks to become generalissimo of the army of Aram (which we know as Syria). That kind of advancement does not happen by accident. Over the years Naaman had distinguished himself as a master strategist. If there was a hill that had to be taken, a battle that had to be won, Naaman would figure out how to do it.

He was also savvy enough to master the political infighting among other generals so as to emerge as the top dog. We're told he was "a great man" in the sight of his master the king and was highly regarded.

We read about Naaman at a high point of his life. He has just defeated the armies of the Israelites and killed their king. He returns home to Aram with unlimited influence, national fame, immense wealth, and unrivaled power.

But he comes back with one other thing: a little patch of discolored skin on his hand. It is the same kind of patch that Father Damien would see thousands of years later, the kind of patch that sent people to Molokai.

This was irony. Naaman can control troops. He holds the life and death of thousands in his hand. He can plan, endure, buy, bribe, or intimidate his way through anything.

Except this. This little patch of discolored skin on his hand is a memo from reality. Reality says that he is a lump of clay walking around on two legs and can't even guarantee his next breath. He had never counted on this.

Actor Clint Eastwood once put it like this: "A man's gotta know his limitations."

In the ancient world the first sign of leprosy was regarded as a death sentence. There is nothing Naaman can do. All his brains, courage, wealth, power, and connections are useless. He's going to die.

God intervenes for the general through the most unlikely source: a slave girl.

GOD SPEAKS THROUGH A SLAVE GIRL

But God intervenes. He does it through the most unlikely source: a slave girl that Naaman brought back with him from Israel.

The slave girl has been dragged away from home, from her mother and father, the people she knows and loves. She has lost all her dreams of marriage and children and home and a life of her own. If Naaman is at the top of the pecking order, she—a female, a slave, a prisoner-of-war—is at the bottom. And Naaman is the man who puts her there.

But God is going to use *her* to save *him*. The life of this all-powerful general rests in the hands of an oppressed slave. She tells Mrs. Naaman, "There is a way. Among my people there is a man named Elisha. He has power from God. He can heal Naaman."

Imagine Naaman's response. Elisha is an Israelite. Israel is the country Naaman has just clobbered. He has just killed their king and who knows how many of their people. For Naaman to go there would be like a Palestine militant looking for medical help in Tel Aviv.

Moreover, it's a slave girl who's telling him what to do. He's not used to taking direction from slave girls. But what else is he going to do? He's desperate. He humbles himself. He does what she says.

He explains his situation to his boss, the king of Aram. The king says, "Okay. I'll write a letter to the king of Israel. It will have to be the new king, since you've killed the old one. (Are you sure this is a good idea, Naaman?)"

The king of Aram doesn't have a clue about how to proceed; he knows nothing of God. He just assumes kings are always in control, so the king of Israel must have control of this magic power to heal. He writes a letter that Naaman delivers to the king: *With this letter I'm sending my servant Naaman so you can cure him of leprosy.* And to butter him up, the general takes along 750 pounds of silver, 150 pounds of gold, and ten sets of clothing for the king.

Now Naaman has hope again. He's got connections — he can use his networks to save his life. He's got wealth — he can use his money to buy back his life.

The king of Israel gets the letter and is not happy about this. He is a corrupt and cowardly king, as was his father. He completely misinterprets this: "The king of Aram is asking me to cure a soldier of leprosy? This is a set-up. Just a pretext to come after me."

All he's thinking about is himself. (One can't help but notice that God doesn't speak much through the VIPs in this story.)

The king tears his robes, an indication of great anguish. He schedules an appointment with the royal therapist. In those days, when kings tore their robes — people got very nervous. Word of this event begins to spread. It gets to Elisha. He tells the king to send Naaman to him.

Naaman goes to Elisha's house, and according to the Bible, it's a pretty impressive motorcade. Horses, chariots, tanks, helicopters — the same horses and chariots that had just helped him kill Israeli soldiers.

Naaman waits for Elisha to come running out of the house. He thinks, "This will be the pinnacle of Elisha's career — that he gets to heal me. This will go to the top of his resume."

GOD SPEAKS THROUGH AN INTERN

Elisha is in the house, sitting in his Barcalounger watching CNN. He doesn't even get out of his chair; instead, he sends out an intern. Naaman, who is used to everyone running to him, is going to hear from God in unexpected ways.

The intern says, "Go, wash yourself seven times in the Jordan, and your flesh will be restored and you will be cleansed."

This is God's message for Naaman, but pride blinds him. *Wash in the Jordan*, he thinks to himself. *This must be some kind of a joke. Who does this Elisha think he is? I thought this would be a major production. He'd come out in person and wave his hands around and pray with a big southern accent—I've seen how this is done on television. I'm a man of great deeds. I'm prepared to do great things for this God—fight his battles, defeat his enemies, present him with great gifts. And now some intern tells me to wash in the Jordan River?*

Naaman doesn't stop there. His belittling goes beyond God and Elisha: *Aren't Abana and Pharpar in my own country better than this muddy little creek?*

Now he's dissing the River Jordan!

"So he turned and went off in a rage," the Bible says. He is offended. The last place he expected to find God was in the Jordan River. He hasn't been treated like a great man at all. He's going to die. But at least his pride's intact.

GOD SPEAKS THROUGH A SERVANT

So God reaches out to Naaman one last time. His servants huddle together: "Who's going to talk to him?" Once more in this story there's folly in high places and God's message comes from a humble spokesman. One of his servants draws the short straw and approaches Naaman nervously (calling him "my father") and states his case.

"If God had asked you to do some great thing," the servant says, "you would do it. If the command had been to win a battle or to give a fortune or to conquer a nation, you would not have hesitated. If God had asked you to do something that would give you an opportunity to demonstrate your greatness and win renown, you would do it. But that's not what God asks. So why not obey God when he asks you to do something small?"

Who knows how long Naaman stands there? On one side are all these years of pride and self-sufficiency and strong-willed achievement and stubborn independence. On the other side is this message, which comes to him from those he least expects. God is *with* Naaman, even though Naaman has done nothing to deserve it. But he doesn't give Naaman a burning bush or a choir of angels. He speaks to him through a slave girl, a prophet's intern, and a lowly servant. God sends his message through people:

"Naaman, I'll meet you—if you'll let me. But I will choose the place. And it's not where you'd expect. I'm not asking you to do something spectacular for me. What I'm going to ask you to do is not glamorous or impressive. You will have to listen for me in the voice of those you think are less smart and powerful than you. You'll have to meet me at the Jordan."

So Naaman goes down to the river. The great general strips off his armor, plunges into the water like a child, splashes up and down seven times, and washes in the Jordan. And there he meets God. He says to Elisha: "Now I know there is no God but this God, the God of Israel."

Blessed are those who know their limitations.

WASHING IN THE JORDAN

Let "washing in the Jordan" stand for all our mundane, non-glamorous interactions with people in our lives: going to meetings, washing the dishes together, reading to a child, listening to a cranky in-law, chatting with a neighbor; doing a bit of business with a clerk at a grocery store, gathering with a small group. "Washing in the Jordan" is how we spend most of life. How well do I do looking for God's presence and listening for his messages in the people who were created in his image?

Jesus is present in his church. When people take his presence there seriously, God moves. John Woolman was a Quaker who felt a strong call by God to work for the abolition of slavery a century before the Civil War. However, he also believed this call needed to be affirmed by his community of faith, many of whom owned slaves. For two years they struggled and wrestled together. In the end they all agreed that God was present in this call, and they said they would support him in his work. As a result of his commitment to God's presence in the church, the Quakers became the first Christian denomination in the New World to take a stand against slavery.

Blessed are those who know their limitations.

God is present in his people. Psychologist Henry Cloud tells about a time in his life when he was wrestling with depression. He asked God for healing. He was hoping for something spectacular, something instantaneous and showy. He thought healing could be something strictly between him and God. Instead, God sent some people to him. He got into a little community of people who loved and cared for him. Over time, their support and truthfulness were used for his healing. There was nothing glamorous about it. God had told him to go wash in the Jordan.

Reflecting on it afterward, Henry said he realized that he had thought the "special effects" route was God's plan A and that people were Plan B. To be healed with a bolt of lightning or some magic words is spectacular; people seem so ordinary. But he realized that with God it is the other way around. People are God's preferred messengers, God's Plan A, because they alone carry his image.

The theological work that perhaps most reflects the spirit of the Sistine Chapel art is called *Oration on the Dignity of Man*, by Giovanni Pico della Mirandola. The *Oration* stresses the creation of human beings as carriers of the divine image. Throughout the Sistine Chapel the faces and bodies of human beings are painted to echo the strength and beauty of God himself. They are "manifestations of human dignity reflecting the divine." Michelangelo himself described human beings as the veils through whom we see God himself:

God, in his grace, shows himself nowhere more
To me, than through some veil, mortal and lovely,
Which I will love for being his mirror.

GOD'S PREFERRED DWELLING PLACE

This doesn't mean, though, that God is particularly present in people whom our society regards as "godlike": the wealthy and beautiful and strong. To the contrary, as one writer puts it, "Jesus frequently chose the humble, poor, rejected, and despised. They are often the preferred dwelling place of God—in them, we may meet God."

A few years ago I went with a group of people, including my teenage daughter, to Honduras on a missions project. One day we went to a kind of mobile medical clinic, which was mostly offering basic hygiene. I looked over at one point and saw my daughter giving shampoos to little Honduran kids who were six or seven years old. After she was done with their hair, Laura would sit down with them and search through their wet, matted hair and pull lice out of it. Even though the water was very cold, they were standing in line, waiting patiently as though this were the highlight of their day, as though someone were giving them a great gift. There is nothing glamorous or impressive about removing lice. Anyone can do it. But if what Jesus said is true, then somehow as Laura was doing that for them, she was doing that for him.

I thought of the world in which we live and what it might be like if we simply served each other in small ways. Mother Teresa was famous for saying that we should not ask to do great things for God, but to do small things with great love. It is hard to withhold love from someone, to be prejudiced against them or cling to resentments or pass judgment, when you're washing hair and pulling out lice. Mother Teresa once told those working with her to be especially tender when they dealt with the poorest of the poor; when they dealt with the dying and the abandoned on the streets of Calcutta. She told them to treat the poor with the kind of reverence with which a priest handles the elements of the Mass. When you touch them, she said, "there you touch Jesus in his distressing disguise."

Jesus is all around me in his distressing disguise. I heard Bishop Desmond Tutu speak once about the relationship between the doctrine of the incarnation and the policy of apartheid. Apartheid, he said, was not simply evil; from a Christian point of view it was also blasphemous. It violated the divine image that God has placed in human beings; it degraded humanity, which Jesus has lifted up by partaking in it.

Mother Teresa said that we should not ask to do great things for God, but to do small things with great love.

I thought of Jesus' parable about the sheep and the goats, which is at its heart a kind of Waldo parable. The King thanks one group of people and condemns another, based on whether or not they gave him food when he was hungry, something to drink when he was thirsty, clothes when he was ragged, and so on. In both cases the people reply in response, "When did we ever see you in such condition?" And the King says, "Whatever you did for the least of these brothers of mine, you did for me." *God is closer than you think.*

So one exercise you might try is to spend a day looking for Jesus in his distressing disguise.

THE CIHU PRAYER

Frank Laubach wrote of a method of continually experiencing God in interactions with other people through what he called the "CIHU" prayer—standing for "Can I help you?"

> One speaks to God and man at the same moment asking "Can I help you get together?" We do not ask "Do I like you" or "Do I need you" or "Do I despise you" but only "Can I help you" and "Can I help you find God."

This one prayer can set a powerful dynamic of God's action in motion.

Some time ago I was visiting my parents and went to get a haircut at a shop they recommended. I started praying this prayer and ended up having a long conversation about God and faith with Ted, the barber. Ted owned the shop along with his wife Joanne, who normally cut my mother's hair.

I told my mom about my conversation with Ted and suggested that the next time she got her hair done, she should talk to Joanne about God. She said no, that she knew a fair amount of Joanne's story; Joanne was on her fifth husband and this was marriage number three for him. They knew how to party and how to spend money, but there was nothing about their life to indicate any openness to God.

"You should talk to her anyway," I said. (You don't often get a chance to tell your mother what to do with such spiritual authority.)

The next time my mom went into the shop, she remembered our conversation as she settled into the chair. "God," she prayed silently, in her own form of the CIHU prayer, "if you want me to talk to Joanne about you, you're going to have to give me some kind of sign, because I don't want to do it."

Joanne's first words to my mom were, "Kathy, I understand that you and your husband have some kind of small group Bible study at your house. Ted and I were wondering if we could come visit it sometime."

My mom took that as a sign.

Joanne began to tell her story. She had grown up in a family that was both alcoholic and abusive. It was also religiously divided: her father was Jewish, and her mother was Catholic. Her dad used to take her to synagogue, then when she got home her mom would send her upstairs with a rosary to ask God to forgive her for going to a Jewish service.

Joanne left home as soon as she could. She was drinking heavily by age sixteen. When she turned twenty-one, she had already been married twice and said she could out-drink any man she knew.

She realized eventually that if she kept going on this way, she would kill herself. She found her way to a meeting of Alcoholics Anonymous. But she struggled with the religious part of the Twelve Steps. She felt a lot of animosity toward the Higher Power that confused her so badly as a girl. She could not bring herself to say the word "God," so she called her higher power "Ralph." She knew no one by that name, so it felt appropriately agnostic. She would say to herself that she had turned her life and will over to Ralph. She was for a time probably the only Ralph-ist in the United States.

Until one day at an AA meeting a man entered the circle who had never attended before. He had obviously been drinking just before coming. He wore skid row clothes and a seedy overcoat, reeked of booze and vomit, and could not walk steadily or speak coherently, but he did get out one statement: "I am an alcoholic. My name is Ralph."

Instead of being amused by the absurdity of this episode, Joanne was crushed. She started to cry, "That's not my God."

After she told my mother that story, Joanne's life turned around. She and Ted began to open their hearts to the presence of God. And it happened. A hair salon became Beth-el, the place where the presence of God became real. God spoke to me through Ted and Ted through me; through me to my mom, through my mom to Joanne and vice versa. In a strange way, he spoke to Joanne through Ralph. He speaks through people.

Your assignment for tomorrow is to look and listen for God in each person whom you see.

So your assignment for tomorrow is to look and listen for God in each person whom you see. When you run into a difficult person, hear Jesus saying, "Love your enemies, and pray for those who persecute you." When you run into a needy person, hear Jesus saying, "Whatever you did for one of the least of these...." When you see someone you love, allow God to love you through them. When someone confronts you, ask God if perhaps he is speaking through them. When you see a stranger, remember the CIHU prayer. When you see a fellow believer, hear Jesus saying, "Where two or three are gathered together in my name, there am I...."

Of all creation, only people are said to be bearers of the image of God. So people have the capacity to be the carriers of his presence like nothing else.

We take long trips to see marvels like the Grand Canyon. Engaged couples plan far ahead so that they can honeymoon at Niagara Falls.

But if our eyes could see clearly, if our hearts were working right, we would fall to the ground in amazement at the sight of a single human being. They are the miracles. They are the God-carriers.

And don't forget, the next time you go into a church, to hold your breath in wonder. What you gaze on is not just a group of people singing songs or listening to a message. It is God's body on earth. Where two or three of them gather in his name, he is there too. It's Waldo Junior.

CHAPTER 7

SPIRITUAL PATHWAYS

Why else were individuals created, but that God, loving all
infinitely, should love each differently?

C. S. Lewis

People are different.

It is bedtime. I go into my daughter's room to tuck her in. She is surrounded by stuffed animals and cherished dolls. She is in that sweet, still, twilight moment between wakefulness and sleep. I sit on the side of her bed, look deeply into her little eyes while she lies there still as if she'd been hypnotized, and try to tell her what is in my heart: "I am so grateful you are alive. Do you have any idea how much I love you? There is no gift in my whole life like the gift of being your dad."

She is staring up at me. Then she speaks: "Daddy, I love you so much...."

Her eyes well up. Mine, too. She puts her little arms around my neck. We are both "feelers," so we savor the emotion. It's a Hallmark moment.

I walk out of the room feeling that I pretty much have the father thing down. I go into the next bedroom. This child, too, is surrounded by animals and dolls, though some of them have been inadvertently kicked to the floor. She is not in that sweet, still, twilight moment, because she does not know twilight. She has only two gears: full throttle and unconsciousness. Her metabolism has an on-off button but no dimmer switch. I sit on the side of her bed, which is not still because she could never hold still long enough to be hypnotized. I go into my same speech: "I am so grateful you are alive. Do you have any idea how much I love you? There is no gift in my whole life like the gift of being your dad."

She is staring up at me, suddenly still. Then she speaks: "Daddy, you've got something hanging out of your nose."

Two children. Same parents, same gene pool, same family, same house—but they have different sets of wiring. Before I became a parent, I had all kinds of naive notions about how much I was going to shape and mold the little lives that would be entrusted to me. After our three children were born, I got educated in a hurry. I realized that if I was going to fully engage my children, I would have to learn to be present with them in ways that would most honor their wiring and personalities. If I tried to force them into all relating to me in the same way, it would be a disaster.

> *Our individual uniqueness means we will all experience God's presence and learn to relate to him in different ways.*

Everyone who is skillful at interacting with people comes to learn this. Successful coaches know which athletes require tongue-lashings to avoid complacency and which need kid-glove treatment to keep from becoming discouraged. Salespeople who make it to the top develop exquisite radar that guides them into knowing which clients want more conversation and which want more space. Effective bosses and therapists and teachers and politicians master the art of reading and responding to human differences.

Not only that, but our lives are much richer because of the diversity of the people in them. I have friends whose greatest joy is to sit down together and have a long talk about a great book. I have other friends whom I have jumped off cliffs with in hang gliding. My friends are present with me in different ways; they see different sides of me. And I'm glad they do!

So why do we think God doesn't know about this?

He is the One who made us, and he made us to be wildly, wonderfully, absurdly different from each other. Thinkers and feelers, backslappers and wannabee hermits, race horses and turtles—"the Lord God made them all."

Yet all too often we fail to realize that our individual uniqueness means we will all experience God's presence and learn to relate to him in different ways, in ways that correspond to the wiring patterns he himself created in us. Frequently in churches we give people a "one-size-fits-all" approach to spiritual growth, like a doctor who prescribes the same medicine for every ailment from rickets to pneumonia. Gary Thomas writes about this:

> All too often, Christians who desire to be fed spiritually are given the same, generic, hopefully all-inclusive methods—usually some variation on a standardized quiet time. Why? Because it's simple, it's generic, and it's easy to hold people accountable to. But, for many Christians, it's just not enough.

God wants to be fully present with each of us. But because he made us to be different from one another, we are not identical in the activities and practices that will help us connect with him. Some writers speak of people as having different spiritual temperaments; Gary Thomas writes of "sacred pathways." (Many authors have written about this over the years; I'm especially indebted to author Gary Thomas; to my former staff colleagues Bill Hybels and Ruth Barton; and to Corinne Ware and Robert Mulholland.)

A spiritual pathway has to do with the way we most naturally sense God's presence and experience spiritual growth. We all have at least one pathway that comes most easily to us. We also have one or two that are the most unnatural and require a lot of stretching for us to pursue.

There is enormous freedom in identifying and embracing your spiritual pathway. It is a little like realizing that if you're an introvert, you don't *have* to work as a salesman; you could get a job in a library. You don't have to beat yourself up or feel guilty because of what is *not* your pathway. You can focus on relating to God in that way for which you were made, while at the same time recognizing your need to stretch in certain areas that don't come as naturally.

We will spend most of this chapter walking through seven spiritual pathways. We need to keep in mind that we all have at least *some* involvement in each one of them. All of us meet God in our minds, at work, in our relationships, and so on. But you will notice that certain pathways most resonate in you. They are the ones that may open up a whole new level of connection between you and God. Yet each pathway has certain dangers attached to it as well, and we will note those too.

INTELLECTUAL PATHWAY

People on the intellectual pathway draw closer to God as they learn more about him. You begin to vibrate when someone talks about the "life of the mind." Ideas are as alive to you as people. You love to study Scripture. The word "theology" has the same impact on you that the phrase "hot doughnuts now" has on the average customer of a Krispy Kreme shop. No one wants to go to a bookstore with you, because once you walk in, they know they're going to miss curfew.

When you go to church, you often find yourself marking time during the musical worship until the sermon starts. You get a little concerned about small groups containing a bunch of people who are just swapping ignorance with each other. When you are faced with crises or spiritual challenges, you tend to go into an analytic, problem-solving mode.

Moses said in the central command of the Law that God's people are to love him "with all your heart and with all your soul and with all your strength." When Jesus cited that statement, he followed the Septuagint (the ancient Greek translation of the Old Testament) by adding one phrase: "with all your heart and with all your soul and with all your strength and with *all your mind*." If you're on the intellectual pathway, you are deeply grateful for that addition. (If it's your dominant pathway, you get a little thrill when you see the word *Septuagint*.)

One person who probably walked this pathway was the apostle Paul. He writes about his life as a student of Gamaliel, one of the great

Jewish scholars of his day. The richness of Paul's mind has occupied many of the greatest thinkers in the world for the past two thousand years. Perhaps most typical of this pathway is how frequently and irresistibly Paul will move in the middle of his writing from *thinking* to *praising*: "Now to him who is able to do immeasurably more than all we ask or imagine, according to his power that is at work within us, to him be glory...."

If you're like Paul, the road to your heart usually runs through your head. You hear God best when you learn. You need to continually immerse yourself in great books, deep thoughts, and sound teaching. When your mind is growing, you feel fully alive. Many of your most significant moments of worship or devotion or decision or repentance came when you were in deep learning mode. You may want to sign up for classes at a seminary or go online for distance learning or get tapes of a few great teachers. If you quit learning, you grow stagnant.

The danger of this pathway lies in becoming all head and no heart. Dallas Willard once observed that it is extremely difficult to be right and not to hurt anybody with it. Very few people enjoy sitting next to the kid in class who's right all the time—and knows it. One of the remarkable things about Jesus is that he was always right, yet never damaged anyone with his mental superiority. "Knowledge puffs up, but love builds up," wrote Paul, who was in a good position to know. So you may want to stretch by making sure your growth in knowledge always leads to a growth in worship.

RELATIONAL PATHWAY

People who follow the relational pathway find that they have a deep sense of God's presence when they're involved in significant relationships. Jesus' statement that "where two or three are gathered together in my name, there am I in the midst of them" makes perfect sense to a relational type. Small groups and other community experiences become indispensable.

Sociologist Robert Wuthnow says that small groups are the biggest social revolution going on in life today, and relational types are one reason why. They are small group junkies. They start small groups at work, in their neighborhood, at school, with their kids' soccer team-mates' parents, and maybe even during long elevator rides.

If this is you, you rarely meet a stranger. When telemarketers call to invite you to refinance your home, you ask them, "How are you—*really?*" Being alone drives you crazy. You sometimes feel guilty when you hear other people speak of long periods of solitude with God. "Solitude wouldn't be so bad," you think to yourself, "if I could just bring a bunch of other *people* along."

> *People who follow the relational pathway find that they have a deep sense of God's presence when they're involved in significant relationships.*

You have often experienced key spiritual moments—being convicted of sin, or encouraged to persevere—as God speaks to you through other people.

I think the apostle Peter may have been on this pathway. He came to Jesus with others. He was part of an inner circle along with James and John. After the crucifixion he was the one who gathered the other disciples to go fishing. The defining moments of his life—his decision to follow Jesus, his confession that Jesus is the Messiah, his denial of Jesus, his caving in to legalists (Paul writes about this in his letter to the Galatians)—all took place in a relational context.

People on this pathway need to lead a relationally rich life. They need to be part of friendships and small groups that are growing in depth and vulnerability. They will discover that they are much more likely to practice prayer or acts of servanthood when they can do it in a relational context. I have a friend on this pathway who was dissatisfied with his prayer life; he volunteered to help lead a prayer group and found that it changed his ability to pray in ways he never could on his own. People on this pathway tend to hear God speak to them more in a conversation than from a book. They stagnate spiritually to the degree they get isolated.

Relational types always have to guard against two dangers. One is superficiality. It is possible to get spread so thin relationally that no one gets past your external self to know you and love you and challenge you deeply. The second is to become dependent on others so that

CHAPTER 7: SPIRITUAL PATHWAYS

you live as a kind of spiritual chameleon. Practices like solitude and silence will be a stretch for you. They may never feel natural, but they will help free you from getting addicted to what others think.

SERVING PATHWAY

On the serving pathway people find that God's presence seems most tangible when they are involved in helping others. Jesus' comment that "whatever you did for the least of these, you did for me" is a truth they experience viscerally. If this is you, you may find that you are somewhat uncomfortable in a setting where you don't have a role to play. But if you can *do* something—set up chairs, make coffee, help decorate—you feel a sense of God's delight in you. You often find yourself making observations that help you grow, or speaking to God in ways that feel most natural while you are engaged in acts of service.

An example of this in Scripture might be a woman named Dorcas. She gets only a brief mention in the book of Acts, but we are told that she was *always* doing good and involved in helping the poor. Mother Teresa would be a kind of modern icon for this pathway. She said that the primary reason she was so involved in serving was not that it was something she was *supposed* to do, but that it brought her joy. She often felt her own inadequacy when she was alone; she never felt the presence of Jesus more strongly than in those she served. Jimmy Carter has probably inspired more people as an ex-president than he did while he was in office because of his passion for servanthood through channels like Habitat for Humanity.

On the serving pathway people find that God's presence seems most tangible when they are involved in helping others.

People on this pathway find that if they are just attending church but have no place to serve, God begins to feel distant. They need to be plugged into a community where they have meaningful serving opportunities. They can enrich their sense of God's presence in their lives by constantly looking for him in the people they serve.

A danger to these people is the temptation to think God is present *only* when they are serving. They can get so caught up in being God's servant they forget they are his child first of all. They will have to stretch by learning to receive love as well as to offer it. Another danger is that if I am a big-time server, there is the temptation to resent others who are not serving as much as I am.

WORSHIP PATHWAY

People on the worship pathway resonate with the psalmist who wrote, "I rejoiced with those who said to me, 'Let us go to the house of the LORD.'" They have a natural gift for expression and celebration. Something deep inside them feels released when praise and adoration are given voice. Some of their most formative moments occur during times of worship.

A classic example of this occurs in Psalm 73. The psalmist is grousing about how often bad people get all the breaks, how the very people his mother warned him about are living the good life, and how he has been keeping his nose clean all his life and it has never paid off. "When I tried to understand all this, it was oppressive to me, till I entered the sanctuary of God."

> *For people on the worship pathway, something deep inside them feels released when praise and adoration are given voice.*

For the psalmist, it was in worship that he *experienced* again the reality of God's presence, and that presence changed his perspective on everything.

If this is you, when you worship at church you hope it will go on for hours. While the intellectual types are looking at their watches, waiting for the message to start, you're internally shouting, "Sing it again!" You may or may not be naturally expressive, but somehow in worship your heart opens up and you come alive. You sometimes find yourself in tears, sometimes in moments of deep joy, because God seems so close.

King David probably had this pathway. He wrote psalms and poetry to God. He played the lyre and expressed his delight in God through music. We are told that on one occasion he danced before the Lord with so much exuberance that he stripped down pretty much to his BVDs in the process—something that you probably don't want to emulate if you are, say, Episcopalian.

If this is your pathway, you need to experience great worship on a regular basis. You may want to turn your car into a rolling sanctuary. Get tapes of great music that helps you worship, then sing your lungs out as you drive down the road. Don't worry that we're all staring at you from our cars. This is how you connect to God. Besides, you will bring joy to all of us who watch.

Here are a few cautions for people on this pathway: Don't judge people who are not as outwardly expressive as you. Some people are from traditions where no one raises a finger, let alone a hand, in a worship service. Not everybody dances. Some of us are Scandinavian.

Also, guard against an experienced-based spirituality that has you always looking for the next "worship high." C. S. Lewis wrote about the fatal sin of saying "encore!" by demanding that God reproduce an experience or an emotion. He said that of all prayers, this may be the one God is least likely to grant, because it can lead us to worship an experience rather than the God to whom our experience points. Music, for instance, can be a great gift to worship. But because music affects our feelings so powerfully I can grow dependent on music to produce a certain emotional response. I may need to spend some time worshiping God *without* music so that my worship is based on who God is and not a matter of getting swept up in certain sounds.

We can begin to judge the worship in our churches superficially by always demanding that they produce a certain emotional response. Engaging in study will be an important stretch for you, so that your heart is deeply rooted in the knowledge of God.

ACTIVIST PATHWAY

If you have an activist pathway, you have a high level of energy. You resonate with statements in Scripture such as the words said of Jesus: "Zeal for your house will consume me." You do zeal. You are a zeal junkie.

You have a passion to act. When you are in a group that hears a story about injustice, other people in the group shake their heads in sadness. You are vibrating for action: "Somebody's gotta *do* something! I'm in. Who's with me?"

Challenges don't discourage you; they energize you. You thrive on opposition. When someone says, "This can't be done," you smile and say, "Watch me!"

You love a fast-paced, problem-filled, complex, strenuous way of life. At the end of the day, you want to be able to say, "I ran really hard. I used every ounce of effort and zeal at my disposal, God, and it's all for you." Activists want to run with everything they have between now and the day they die, which will probably be in their early fifties of a heart attack. And when they get to the other side, they are desperately hoping heaven does not consist just of a cloud, a harp, a nice house, and an eternal songbook. That sounds a lot more like eternal punishment to them.

> If you have an activist pathway, challenges don't discourage you; they energize you.

One biblical example of an activist is Nehemiah. When he hears that his beloved Jerusalem has fallen into disrepair, he is upset and wants to act. He invokes a classic example of the Activist Prayer: "I prayed to my God and said to the king ..." For activists, prayer and action naturally go together. They are triggered to look for and depend on God's presence and guidance in the heat of battle.

If you are an activist, you need a cause. It doesn't have to be glamorous or visible, but it has to demand the best you have to offer. Without this, your spiritual life will stagnate.

A caution for you is that you may get so excited about the cause that you begin to run over other people or exploit them because you get so focused on what you want to accomplish. Even God may become a means to an end for you rather than the one you serve. Activists sometimes have a hard time discerning God's true call from their own strong impulses to action. You may need to create balance by spending time in solitude and reflection, so that you allow God to speak to you about what is truly motivating your action.

CONTEMPLATIVE PATHWAY

If you have a contemplative pathway, you love large blocks of uninterrupted time alone. It is very likely that when you were a child, your parents used to tell you to get outside and play with other kids more. Reflection comes naturally to you. You often feel like an observer in life.

God is most present to you when distractions and noises are removed. Images and metaphors and pictures help you as you pray. If you get too busy, or spend too much time with too many people hanging around, you begin to feel drained and stretched thin.

This is a challenge in American society. What happens when a quiet contemplative type meets a chatty relational type? They get married. And drive each other crazy. The contemplative says, "Don't you have any depth at all? All you ever want to do is schmooze!" The relational type says, "Don't you even care about people? You just want to navel-gaze all the time!"

If you have a contemplative pathway, you love large blocks of uninterrupted time alone.

There's an interesting difference between the activist and the contemplative. When an activist says, "I'll call you back," that means, "I'll call you back as soon as I get home, if not sooner because I do have a cell phone with me at all times." When a contemplative says, "I'll call you back," it means, "I'll call you back before I die. Probably right before."

The apostle John—who was known as the disciple that Jesus loved—has been understood to be one who loved to bask in the adoration of God. People like this are often sought out because of their great wisdom and sense of poise.

If you are a contemplative, you may need *permission* to follow your pathway. American society tends to value networkers and activists; contemplatives don't end up on many magazine covers. You have what

Gordon MacDonald calls a "large interior world," or intrapersonal communication. You do not require much external stimulation. Making time to listen to God in silence and solitude is vital to the health of your soul, and necessary for you to experience a deepening sense of his presence. You will need regular, protected, intense, undistracted times alone.

Reading other contemplatives, such as St. John of the Cross or Henri Nouwen, often helps you. You will probably find it helpful to keep a journal. (Relational types almost never journal. They might dictate to a stenographer. Activists don't journal much, though they may sell other peoples' journals.)

You may need to stretch in the area of relationships. It will be tempting for you to retreat to your inner world when friends or work or society disappoints you. Involvement in significant relationships and regular acts of service will help keep you tethered to the external world.

CREATION PATHWAY

Creation types find that they have a passionate ability to connect with God when they are experiencing the world he made. In Greek mythology there is a character named Antaeus, who could not be defeated in wrestling as long as he was touching mother earth. (Hercules killed him after holding him in midair.) For people on the creation pathway, there is something deeply life-giving and God-breathed about nature. Being outdoors replenishes and energizes you. If you are cooped up inside too long, your soul starts to feel stale.

For people on the creation pathway, there is something deeply life-giving and God-breathed about nature.

We are told that "the heavens declare the glory of God," and that glory shines out of all creatures great and small. People on this pathway not only see God in the spectacular—Niagara Falls, or the Grand Canyon—but trace his presence in a leaf dropping from an oak tree in autumn, in a zephyr breeze on a summer day, or in the liquid song of a wren.

Being out in the creation opens your spirit to God. Naturalist John Muir called nature "the manuscripts of God."

We see in Scripture how Jesus illustrates this pathway (and probably all the other pathways as well). He was constantly withdrawing from people to go up into the mountains or to be near a lake, and there to commune with his Father. He wanted to be out in the creation—which I suppose is not surprising, since he created it!

In Jesus' day, of course, being outdoors was much more a part of life for people automatically than it is for many of us today. We can spend a whole day without even looking at the sky. But if creation is your pathway, you will want to spend large chunks of time outdoors. It will often be particularly helpful to have times of prayer or meditation in nature. (Both Jesus' teachings and the psalms are rich with passages that demonstrate much time meditating on how we learn about God from creation: trees and seeds and sparrows and leviathans and mountains of refuge and rivers of living water.) This may be a challenge, depending on where you live. You may need to bring beauty inside during certain parts of the year; if you do, arrange to have flowers or the flame of a candle nearby as you pray.

People on the creation pathway may need to guard against using it as an escape. People are part of creation too—but you may find that when they disappoint you, you are tempted to run away to the woods. Folks in our day are sometimes prone to think, "I don't need church; I can worship God on my own in nature." But of course, we have to learn to see beauty where God does, and people are the most valued part of all that he created.

USING THE PATHWAYS TO EXPERIENCE GOD

Once we know which pathways are ours, how do we use this information to help us experience God's closeness? For starters, we need to accept and embrace the unique way God created us. Instead of following "mass production" approaches to spiritual growth, we need to make sure that we spend adequate time and activity pursuing the pathways that most help us connect with God. Understand and build on your pathways. Take a look through these descriptions, and try to assess which ones you most naturally follow. Make sure you incorporate practices that involve these pathways into the rhythms of your life. This will probably take repeated attempts and experimentation. Celebrate that this is part of how God made you and wants to connect with you.

Embracing how God made you also means you need to resist the temptation to envy somebody else's pathway. For instance, if you are a contemplative, you may see some high-profile activist whom many people admire and wish you were more like that person. You may begin to doubt that the way you are wired up is such a good thing: *The activists are the ones who get all the recognition in this world. I guess I'll always be second-class.* Ironically, it is when you honor your pathway—when you spend time alone with God in reflection—that you are most likely to embrace what God made you to be.

By contrast, beware the temptation to judge somebody else's pathway. I know of a contemplative man who is married to a relational woman, who doesn't spend nearly as much time in solitude or quiet prayer as he does. It is easy for him to assume an air of superiority: *How come you can't get your prayer life together? Why don't you go at prayer as long and hard as I do?* But of course, the greatest single gift we can pray for is love. And when it comes to love, she beats him on every lap around the track. No pathway is superior to any other.

We also need to pay attention to those pathways that may not come naturally to us. It is important that we have some involvement in *each* of the pathways. No one can ignore their intellectual life or opt out of worship. And each of us has a few temptations that will mean there are pathways we particularly need to be stretched in. For instance, you might be tempted to think, *No wonder I don't like to be alone. I'm a relational type. Now I'm off the hook for solitude—I don't have to do that at all!*

Not a good idea. Because one of the temptations of relational types is to be overly influenced by others, solitude is an important stretching experience. It may never come naturally to you. But it will help you to keep from living as a chameleon.

God is closer than you think. One of the greatest dimensions of this truth is that God wants to have a relationship with you that is unlike his relationship with any other being in all creation. In the book of Revelation, John writes that one day we will each receive from God a name that remains a secret between him and us throughout eternity. C. S. Lewis writes,

> What shall we take this secrecy to mean? Surely, that each of the redeemed shall forever know and praise some one aspect of the Divine beauty better than any other creature can. Why else were individuals created, but that God, loving all infinitely, should love each differently? ... If all experienced God in the same way and returned Him an identical worship, the song of the Church triumphant would have no symphony, it would be like an orchestra in which all the instruments played the same note.

My grandmother said it better, I think. When anyone asked her which of her six children she loved the most, she said love for your children doesn't work that way. She said it's as if when each child is born, another little room gets added to your heart. And no one else occupies that room. It doesn't have to be bigger or better than any other room. It's just *theirs*.

"In my Father's house are many rooms," Jesus said. One of them was added on when you became his child. That one is yours, and no one else can ever occupy it. It is secret to you and him. It's your own private Sistine Chapel. It is furnished by every moment of intimacy and wonder and togetherness shared by you and your Father.

In the whole divine journey, no one else can walk your pathway. In the whole cosmic choir, no one else can sing your song.

CHAPTER 8

"AS YOU WISH"

*What matters, what Heaven desires and Hell fears, is precisely
that further step, out of our depth, out of our own control.*

C. S. Lewis

On the bookshelf of my daughter Mallory's bedroom sits a volume called *The Princess Bride*. It was the basis of a quirky little movie that my family has seen more times than I can count. It comes from the pen of William Goldman, though he pretends he just translated it from a Florinese manuscript by an S. Morgenstern that set records for the most weeks on a Florinese bestseller list. It took a long time to convince my daughter that there was no S. Morgenstern, no Florinese language, and, sadly, no country named Florin.

A friend of mine named Gary Moon writes that his family has seen the movie so often they have memorized large chunks of the dialogue. When he loses a tennis match, he is likely to smile slyly and say under his breath, *But I know a secret you do not know. I am not right-handed.*

Gary is not the only one with a memory. When my children were growing up, they would amuse themselves for hours in the backseat of the car by quoting favorite sections:

—No more rhyming now, I mean it.

—Anybody want a peanut?

I was once at a Christmas concert performed by singer Fernando Ortega. When he started to speak, we were all expecting some traditional holiday greeting; instead his first words were, "My name is Fernando Ortega. You kill-ed my father. Prepare to die!"

And I have been offered substantial amounts of money (Okay, five dollars) to begin a wedding ceremony by impersonating the very impressive Archdeacon of Florin, who stands on the platform of an ornate cathedral, is dressed in imposing robes and vestments, and follows the glorious thunder-blasts of organ music by saying in a voice that sounds almost exactly like Elmer Fudd, "Mah-widge. Mah-widge is what bwings us heah today ... that dweam wiffin a dweam...."

Some of the lines are profoundly existential. In one scene a mysterious man in black is besting a great swordsman in a duel. The swordsman is beside himself with curiosity to know the identity of his brilliant foe:

—Who are you?

—No one of importance. A lover of the blade, like yourself.

—I *must* know.

—Get used to disappointment.

Sounds like something from the book of Ecclesiastes: "Vanity of vanities; all is vanity...." Life is "meaningless, a chasing after the wind." Get used to disappointment.

AS YOU WISH

But there is one line that lies at the heart of the book's story—and at the heart of your story as well. It is spoken when the story begins and when it ends. It is a kind of prayer. In fact, it is the greatest prayer Jesus himself ever prayed. If we were ever able to pray it truly and continually, it is in a real sense the only prayer you and I would ever need. Gary Moon tells it this way:

> As the movie opens, we see the heroine going about chores on a farm. Her name is Buttercup. (I know, but I still

like the movie.) Soon we meet a young man who works on the farm and answers to the name Farm Boy.

Whenever Buttercup asks Farm Boy to do something for her, he always replies, "As you wish." That's all he ever says to her.

As they grow into their hormones, Buttercup seems to be developing a crush on Farm Boy. One day as he is about to leave the room, she asks him to fetch her a pitcher, which is within easy reach for her. Farm Boy walks over, then stares into her eyes, lifts the pitcher, and whispers: "As you wish."

In that moment, returning his gaze, Buttercup realizes that every time he has said, "As you wish," he was really saying, "I love you."

For many centuries, those wisest among us about the spiritual life have insisted that this one line is the door that opens the heart to the presence of God. There is no greater expression of love than a freely submitted will. *As you wish.*

Jean Pierre de Caussade writes, "Every moment, and in respect of everything, we must say like St. Paul, 'Lord, what should I do?' Let me do everything you wish."

There is no greater expression of love than a freely submitted will. As you wish.

Jesus said, "As the Father has loved me, so I have loved you. If you keep my commandments, you will abide in my love, just as I have kept my Father's commandments and abide in his love."

Brother Lawrence writes, "Let us often remember, dear friend, that our sole occupation in life is to please God."

"At the heart of communion with God," writes Gary Moon, "is the whisper, 'As you wish.'"

There are moments when I remember to pray that prayer. They are not usually dramatic. The tax man emails us with the good news that Uncle Sam is sending back some of our money, and it occurs to me that I could be generous with it. I'm sitting in a meeting at work,

GOD IS CLOSER THAN YOU THINK

and the thought strikes my mind that I could be quiet for a few minutes and look for someone else's idea to cheer on. I've been traveling for a week and I'm in a strange airport and I'm feeling lonely, and I get a sudden impulse to open the Bible and ask God to meet with me there. And he does.

There are other times when it doesn't even enter my mind to say, "As you wish." I'm not necessarily being defiant, just oblivious. There are times when I'm not sure *what* God wishes me to do, and I have to just muddle through on my own. And there are times when I simply don't want to pray it—when I choose to *not* pray it.

C. S. Lewis wrote that the day is coming when every soul will adopt one of two postures before God: either joyful surrender or defiant separation. One day every being will say either "Thy will be done," or "*My* will be done." And the reality is that—at least to some small degree—our hearts are always assuming one or the other of these postures. From one moment to the next we make choices: What will I do next? How will I treat this person? What will I do with this money? Where will I allow this temptation to lead me?

The heart that learns to say, "As you wish," from one moment to the next opens itself to the Power of the Universe. It does not matter whether our task is great or small or whether we are famous or obscure. Anne Lamott has a wonderful thought: "The Gulf Stream can pass through a straw; if the straw aligns itself with the Gulf Stream."

CONDUCTORS AND RESISTERS

An analogy from the field of electricity can help us think about our response to God. The difference between a conductor and a resistor can be put like this: a conductor is willing to let go. Floating around the periphery of its atoms are electrons that can quite easily pass from one atom to another. They are more or less free agents. So a conductor has what we might call a generosity of spirit when it comes to electrons. In previous times writers used to speak of this as a sense of detachment. Ignatius of Loyola said we are to cultivate a sense of indifference. The idea is not that we should seek to be apathetic about all our circumstances. Instead, it is that our deepest desire is for God and his kind of life, and every other desire has to take a backseat to this one absolute quest.

A resister, by contrast, does not want to let go. It hangs onto its little electrons. It clings to the status quo. It is afraid to let go because it wants to keep its little possessions intact. And so it does. But the resister never knows much power.

The secret of the conductor is that it is not generating its own power. The conductor is not particularly strong or clever; it is simply a conduit. It is open and receptive to the flow of current that can change the world from darkness to light.

The resister's prayer is, "Leave me alone."

The conductor's prayer is, "As you wish."

Each prayer gets answered.

We live in a spiritually charged universe. The flow of the Holy Spirit is all around us. We did not invent it, but it has now become fully available. Jesus once said, "Whoever believes in me, as Scripture has said, streams of living water will flow from within them." John's gospel explains that Jesus was talking about the Spirit.

We do not have much power in our wills, but we can choose whether we will be resisters or conductors.

We do not have much power in our wills, but we can choose whether we will be resisters or conductors. And our prayer will be answered.

It is striking how often resistors and conductors get paired up in Scripture. Often the people with the greatest outward power are the ones who resist, and those who look less significant end up being the conduits. Pharaoh was a resistor: God's power could have flowed through him, but he said no. Moses was a conductor: he had many inadequacies and shortcomings, but from the burning bush to his final moments on Mount Pisgah, where he looked out over the Promised Land, he learned to say, "As you wish."

King Saul was an impressive man, head and shoulders above the crowd, but he shut his heart from the flow. David was very human, embarrassingly fallible, but the flow of the Spirit through him was at times incandescent. Haman had the power, humanly speaking, but his hostile heart was a circuit-breaker. Esther—a woman regarded as just a pretty ornament by the king and those in power—was a bolt of lightning.

Herod was called "the Great," but he held tight to his throne and resisted the Messiah. John the Baptist was a hermit in the desert, but in his self-abandonment ("I must decrease") a power flowed that even his beheading could not stem.

The ultimate conductor, of course, was Jesus himself. Frank Laubach notes that forty-seven times in the gospel of John alone Jesus said he was "under God's orders" and that he did and said everything his Father commanded. "He was listening every moment of the day to His invisible companion and saying, 'Yes.'"

THE GLOW OF THE PICKLE

I did an electrical experiment in church one time. I brought in a scientist with a Ph.D. so that if someone got electrocuted, it wouldn't be me. We turned off all the lights, hooked up an ordinary pickle to some wires, then passed an electrical current through it. The pickle glowed. It gave light to a room with thousands of people. It was not a huge amount of light—not enough to read by. But there was light.

If God can make a pickle glow, what can he do through you?

Many people believe that the flow of the Holy Spirit is reserved for spiritual giants like Mother Teresa or Billy Graham. But throughout history God has caused his power to flow through the most unlikely people: a prostitute named Rahab, a con man named Jacob, a cheat named Zacchaeus.

This was the miracle of the early church. As the believers met for prayer, "the place where they were meeting was shaken. And they were all filled with the Holy Spirit," because the ordinary becomes extraordinary when filled with the power of God.

So the next time you feel inadequate or not very gifted, remember that even a pickle can glow if it stays plugged in to the flow. Remember: "The Gulf Stream can pass through a straw; if the straw aligns itself with the Gulf Stream."

It is God's job to send the flow of the Spirit into our lives. When we have thoughts that prompt us toward the fruit of the Spirit—promptings to express love to someone, celebrations of inner joy, the conviction that we are at peace—these are all surges of the Spirit's current. My job, in a sense, is simply to offer the surrender of a conductor. *As you wish.*

THE SURRENDER OF OBEDIENCE

Not long ago I was traveling overseas. When I was settling into my hotel room, I noticed that the television remote control listed a bunch of conventional settings and then listed one "adults only" channel that was available free of charge. Its not uncommon for hotels to offer adult movies that require an extra billing, but I had not often seen a case where a channel like that was offered for free. Somehow, the fact that it could be viewed for no money, without anybody knowing, was unsettling for me. The thought came to me that I should talk about this with one of the men who was on this trip with me, and ask him to check in with me the next day and hold me accountable not to watch the channel.

I immediately went into resistance mode. *I don't think I need to do this. It would be embarrassing to me. I don't know this guy very well—I don't want him thinking I'm some kind of impulse-ridden wacko.*

I fought the idea through most of the afternoon and even when I saw the man at dinner. But I could not shake the thought. So at dessert I told him about it and asked him to pray. I felt kind of sheepish about the whole thing.

The next morning I saw the man at breakfast, and he asked to meet with me. He asked me how the night had gone, and I told him there was no problem. He then went on to talk with me about a vulnerable issue in *his* life that we would never have discussed if I hadn't taken a first step of vulnerability the night before (even though I took it kicking and screaming). God used this man in my life, and me in his, in a way that neither of us could have foreseen on our own. "The wind blows where it will. . . ."

This lesson is one of the great secrets of Twelve Step programs. When I try to handle temptation through my willpower, I am doomed to failure, because I'm restricted to my little strength. I am a resister. But when I acknowledge my powerlessness and turn my will over to God, I am aligning with the Gulf Stream. *As you wish.*

THE SURRENDER OF SERVANTHOOD

Last month I was sitting in my office, writing a sermon on servanthood: "Whatever you do for the least of these ... you do for me." It was vacation week for high school students. My daughter Mallory called me. She was cooking dinner, a very exotic recipe for duck, which I love.

"Dad, could you stop by a store and pick up a couple of things I can't get?"

My immediate response: "No, I can't do that. I've got to write this message about how important it is to serve; I've got to convince people to set aside their petty agendas and get off their little ladders and do acts of service for others—

"I don't have time to go to the store for you. How come you can't get it?"

"Because the recipe calls for cognac and Grand Marnier," said my seventeen-year-old daughter.

Oh.

I go to the very nice gourmet grocery store across the street from my church. I'm in a hurry and can't find the right stuff. I feel a little awkward about asking for help, because even though I work at a Presbyterian church, I'm still viewed as a teetotaler. I finally find someone who works there.

"I need cognac and Grand Marnier," I tell him, "but just very small bottles of them. It's not for me. It's for my teenage daughter."

And the store clerk replied: *As you wish.*

THE SURRENDER OF PAYING ATTENTION

There is a passage in a book by George MacDonald that expresses very well a spiritual truth that can be hard to articulate. One of the characters is a young man, not far from death, who is in the process of seeking God. He is speaking with his spiritual mentor. At one point in their time together there is a long silence. The young man plucks a pale-red pimpernel from the ground and, struck by its beauty, suddenly finds himself in tears. He feels embarrassed at this expression of emotion over something as small as a flower.

Don't be surprised, his friend tells him. This merely shows that "all about us, in earth and air, wherever eye or ear can reach there is a power ever breathing itself forth in signs, now in a daisy, now in the wind, in a cloud, in sunset...." Then MacDonald writes this insightful line: "that the same God who is in us,... also is all about us—inside, the Spirit; outside, the Word. And the two are ever trying to meet in us."

The same God who is within us is also all about us. He is not restricted to church and the Bible.

The same God who is within us is also all about us. He is in Bible readings and church services, but he is not restricted to those places. When we see beauty that overwhelms us; when we see acts of compassion that make us choke up; when we feel longing so deep and sweet that everything else in our life recedes; when the turn of a phrase or a bar of music catches us off guard and takes our breath away—then perhaps it is something more than just an aesthetic experience. Then it is God within us, indwelling every cell in our body, calling out for us to see and open ourselves up to his presence all around us.

"Deep calls to deep in the roar of your waterfalls," is how the psalmist puts it. When we stand before a waterfall that thunders down a cliff, we can actually feel deep in our chest the vibrations of the water going over the falls. This is a beautiful picture of what is happening all over creation. The depths of the presence of God around us are crying out to the depths of our souls—where he also resides. *Deep calls to deep.... And the two are ever trying to meet in us.*

Our task, in order to stay in the flow of God's presence, is to pay attention. To refuse the blindness that comes with self-preoccupation. To allow the God who is in us to point to and rejoice in his presence all around us. To ask him to keep us from sleepwalking through his world; to refuse to give in to a pace of life that reduces his handiwork to a blur.

As the artist Georgia O'Keeffe put it, "Nobody sees a flower—really—it is so small it takes time—we haven't time—and to see takes time, like to have a friend takes time."

The same God who is in us also is all about us. We do not even need to hunt for him. We only need to open our eyes. "We are here to abet Creation and to witness it, to notice each thing, so each thing gets noticed .... so that Creation need not play to an empty house," writes Anne Dillard.

Sometimes as I walk through my day I will pause and say a prayer with my palms facing up, as a way of expressing to God my openness to his presence and direction in this moment. *As you wish.*

ONE THING SURRENDER IS NOT

Before we look at a last form of surrender, I want to address one potential misunderstanding that has crushed many people's spirits. It is this: The call to surrender does not mean we are supposed to kill off all our desires.

God created desire. In his original plan, desires are an indicator of a creature's purpose. God made birds with a longing to fly, fish with a reflex to swim, and beavers with an itch to build water-homes.

All too often, what gets presented as a state of surrender to God looks more like the *absence* of life than its fulfillment. John Steinbeck writes about such a character in *East of Eden:*

> *All too often, what gets presented as a state of surrender to God looks more like the absence of life than its fulfillment.*

"George was a sinless boy, and grew to be a sinless man. No crime of commission was ever attributed to him, and his crimes of omission were only misdemeanors. In his middle life it was discovered that he had pernicious anemia. It is possible that his virtue lived on a lack of energy."

At the end of the book of Ecclesiastes is a passage that speaks of the goodness of desire.

The writer advises us to learn to love God now, in the days of strength and vigor, before the "days of trouble" come. He describes the "days of trouble" with a series of very colorful metaphors.

> When the grinders cease because they are few,
>   and those looking through the windows grow dim;...
> when men rise up at the sound of birds,
>   but all their songs grow faint;
> when ... the grasshopper drags himself along
>   and desire no longer is stirred....

Notice that the writer doesn't say we should look forward to the loss of desire. This passage does not picture spiritual maturity. It portrays decrepitude—what happens when people turn (fill in an age) and their body starts falling apart.

An old Quaker sect taught that the way to know a "call" is from God is that it is *always* contrary to your desire. Some Quakers actually walked naked in the streets because it was "contrary to their own will or inclination" and, therefore, "in obedience to the Lord."

The capacity for desire is itself a gift from God. His original plan was that our desires be strong and passionate—and coincide perfectly with his will for us. But because our desires have been poisoned by sin, they are not fully reliable guides. We have always to be willing to sacrifice less worthy desires for greater ones.

American culture says that real life requires the gratification of our desires. Many people try to convince us that we are essentially like the Sesame Street Cookie Monster. It has a very simple philosophy of life: see cookie, want cookie, eat cookie. Appetites exist to be gratified.

Distorted spirituality says real life requires the elimination of our desires. The religion that most tends to be associated with the renunciation of all desire is Buddhism (even though, ironically, most statues of the Buddha that we see in America make him look as if he had a thing for cookies).

Jesus says that real life requires the transformation of our desires. If you are thirsty—if you have unsatisfied desires—"come to me."

135

Desire itself is an invitation to seek God's presence. As C. S. Lewis once wrote, "Indeed, if we consider ... the staggering nature of the rewards promised in the Gospels, it would seem that Our Lord finds our desires, not too strong, but too weak....We are far too easily pleased."

THE SURRENDER OF OUR FAILURES

Sometimes we forget to surrender. Sometimes we refuse. Then our sense of guilt and inadequacy can cut us off from the current of God's presence. On the occasions when we have failed to surrender, then we have to learn to surrender even our failure.

The most important thing about failure is this: Even when we have failed, the flow of the Spirit can be restored in our lives at any moment. Right now. All we have to do is ask.

Since my family moved to northern California, we have become surfing addicts. Actually, my son is the addict; I am more or less an enabler. I am not at all good at surfing. I fall off the board a lot. I spend much of my time in the water looking around for sharks. (Stay away from beaches that have lots of seals. If you're in the water with seals and you're wearing a wet suit, to a shark you're just the slowest-moving seal.)

But the good news about surfing is this: If you miss one wave, if you fall off, if you wipe out, there's another wave coming right behind it. God just keeps sending them. He never runs out of waves. He has an inexhaustible supply. He's like a wave machine.

The Bible's word for that is "grace."

It works this way:

I stopped at a gas station, but was in a hurry to get to work. The car in another lane was leaving. The right-of-way was not real clear. He cut in front of me.

I felt a surge of anger that shocked me. He looked at me; I looked at him.

He started gesturing, with intense hostility in his face. Mine, too.

I gestured back—differently, because I'm a pastor. I'm thinking, *Get out of my way. Don't you know I have to get to the office, write a book about how to flow with the Spirit of God every moment of your life?* (Starting to see a pattern? I'm a slow learner.)

When my car pulled into the street, I could feel it in my belly that—for that little exchange—I had extinguished any kind of sensitivity to the Spirit's presence or guidance in my mind.

I had—at least for those several seconds—completely shut myself off to the flow of the Spirit. I was a resistor instead of a conductor. I had broken the circuit.

But my failure doesn't get the last word.

For then I say, as I've said a thousand times before, "God, I'm sorry. I don't want to live that kind of life. I don't want to be that kind of person. Forgive me. Help me try again."

And Jesus says to me again the words that are his specialty, the words he himself cried out to his Father from the garden of Gethsemane, the words that death itself cannot stop. They are the same words by which the Princess Bride finally recognizes her true love, the words that can align a straw to the Gulf Stream.

As you wish.

CHAPTER 9

WHEN GOD SEEMS ABSENT

This eternal fountain is hidden deep,
Well I know where it has its spring,
Though it is night!

St. John of the Cross

My friend Nancy Beach once taught a series on spiritual life in which she compared our varying experiences of God's presence to the seasons of the year. She gave eloquent descriptions of the beauty and wonder of spring, summer, and fall. When it came to the topic of the soul in winter, however, she asked me to take her place. So I thought I would start this chapter with words I associate with winter.

Death. Ice. Hypothermia. Windchill.

Snow. Shoveling snow. Shoveling more snow. Buying a snowblower.

Salt trucks. Black ice. Dead batteries. Frostbite. Gangrene. Thermal underwear. My wife wearing long thermal underwear for months at a time.

Ice fishing. Diminished mental capacity.

Seasonal affective disorder. Happy days for electrical utility companies.

Recreational eating.

Death.

I don't like winter.

I know there are people in the world who claim to love winter. But it always makes me wonder: How many people spend their working careers in Florida, then retire and move to Minot, North Dakota?

I have heard people say, "But God made winter—it must be good."

There is no mention of winter in the Bible before the Fall. In Genesis we read about trees bursting with fruit and rivers flowing with water and people who didn't even need clothes. Wherever the Garden of Eden was, it clearly was not Milwaukee in January.

The Bible tells us that winter came because someone once did something very, very bad. People have been paying for it ever since. I speak from experience. I lived for a decade in Chicago, which was founded when a group of people from New York said, "The crime and the poverty are good, but we'd like it colder."

A WINTRY SPIRITUALITY

Regardless of what you may feel about the meteorological season, I want us to think about a kind of winter of the soul. Spiritual winter.

You may be able to relocate to some part of the world where you can avoid cold weather, but there is no place you can move to escape spiritual winter.

You may relocate to some part of the world to avoid cold weather, but you cannot escape spiritual winter.

Theologian Martin E. Marty wrote a book of reflections about the terminal illness and loss of his beloved wife. He said one of the resources human beings need is what he calls "a wintry spirituality" for times when the warmth and joy is taken away from us and a sunny disposition is not enough to bring them back. We need a way of holding on to God when it feels as if God has let go of us.

Winter may come when someone has lost a job or experienced vocational failure. They feel a deep sense of sadness, even shame. They are not sure, without this job, who they are anymore.

Winter may arrive the day the word comes back from the doctor's lab that the test was positive. All the dreams you took for granted —that you will watch your kids grow up and get married, that you will grow old with your spouse and die when you're good and ready—suddenly torture you with the thought that you won't be there to see them fulfilled.

Maybe winter comes when you feel as if you have failed as a parent. Or it arrives the day someone you loved with your whole heart has died. You prayed so hard, you hoped so much, you don't understand.

Any of these events may chill the soul. Any of them may announce the onset of winter. But they are not its worst feature. The hardest part of winter is that God seems gone.

> I cry to you for help, O LORD;
> in the morning my prayer comes before you.
> Why, O LORD, do you reject me
> and hide your face from me?

It is the aversion of God's face, what feels like his absence, that is the psalmist's greatest pain. C. S. Lewis wrote after the death of his wife, "Where is God?... Go to Him when your need is desperate, when all other help is vain, and what do you find? A door slammed in your face, and a sound of bolting and double bolting on the inside. After that, silence."

This is the hardest part of winter of the soul. It's not just this or that bad event.

We can't find God. He doesn't answer. "Why do you reject me? Why do you hide your face?"

JOB AND THE ABSENCE OF GOD

Certain books of the Bible—Ecclesiastes, Lamentations, and many of the psalms—are wintry books. But in all human history, no one has embodied winter more than a man named Job. In his book we come to the page where Waldo is hardest to find.

The story begins, "In the land of Uz there lived a man whose name was Job." The reader has to try to figure out where Uz was. The directions are deliberately vague: "He was the greatest man among all the people of the East." The writer's point is that Job is not a part of Israel. You could put the setting like this: "A long time ago, in a place far, far away...."

The problems in this book are the problems of the human race. All of us will wrestle at some time with the absence of God.

In the beginning everything is as we think it should be. Job is "blameless and upright, a man who fears God and shuns evil." He is so cautious he even offers daily sacrifices for his children—"just in case," he thinks. Maybe they sinned. Maybe God is easily offended.

God gives him a wonderful life. The amount of blessing he experiences is directly proportional to the amount of obedience he offers.

But winter is coming to Uz. Uz will be a place where very bad things happen to a very good man. Uz will be a place, not just where suffering comes, but where it comes without warning and without explanation, creating confusion and despair.

Then suddenly in the story there's a radical shift in scenery. There is a dispute between Satan and God, and Satan is allowed to wreak havoc on Job's life. Philip Yancey notes that the writer sets up this book like a play, but the action is going on in two locations. Picture a theater with two stages; a lower stage and an upper stage.

This is crucial to the story: We know what is going on in both settings, but the characters on earth do not. All they can see is what's happening on earth. All Job knows is that he has lost his livestock, his wealth, his servants, and his children. We wait to see his response.

He grieves. He worships. He falls to the ground. He cries, "May the name of the LORD be praised." In all this, he "did not sin."

We switch back to the upper stage for one more brief conversation. At first glance, the action in heaven looks very strange. It looks like a cosmic wager between God and Satan, where God uses Job and his family as pawns to win a bet. But it's not.

The key question on the upper stage—in fact, the key question to the whole book—comes when Satan asks, "Does Job fear God for nothing?"

In other words, Satan is saying, "Job is devoted to you and worships you because it is in his self-interest. Quid pro quo." Satan is charging God with being naive. "You think Job loves you. The truth is, he loves you the way children love the ice cream man; the way aging actresses love Botox. Turn off the faucet of blessing and watch how fast he turns off the faucet of devotion."

> *The question is, can a human being hold on to God in the face of suffering?*

The question is, can a human being hold on to God in the face of suffering? After all, suffering is the test of love.

So Job gets hit with a second wave of trouble. This time there are some subtle differences in his response. He does not fall to the ground in worship. He does not say, "The name of the LORD be praised."

He goes to sit on an ash heap at the town dump. Maybe it is an act of grieving. Maybe he is being isolated because his skin condition—part of his suffering—could be leprosy.

Job's wife says, "Curse God and die!" This cannot be encouraging to Job. This does not sound like Dale Carnegie. But Job's wife, too, has lost all she had, including her children. She will now have to care for a horribly diseased husband until he dies, then she will be left alone and destitute. She gives voice to thoughts that have surely occurred to Job.

Job doesn't curse God. But notice what he says: "Shall we accept good from God, and not trouble?" He is struggling to understand God now. Is God the kind of person who sends evil? Is God really good?

The writer says, "In all this, Job did not sin *in what he said*." After the first wave, the text simply says, "In all this Job did not sin."

So now there is a little qualification. "Job did not sin *in what he said*." In his heart, Job has begun to struggle.

FRIENDS IN WINTER

Then Job's friends hear about all the troubles that have come upon him—Eliphaz the Temanite, Bildad the Shuhite, Zophar the

Naamathite. (Not mentioned is Dadgum the termite.) These friends meet together to go and sympathize with Job and give him comfort.

Job used to be famous for his wealth and greatness. Now he's famous for his problems and suffering. These friends are going to *"sympathize with him...."* The Hebrew verb *nud* refers to body movement—shaking back and forth, nodding the head. We see this sometimes when people experience trauma and go into shock, rocking themselves back and forth like a mother with a baby.

The friends' love is so strong, their grief is so great, that they plan to sit next to him and take on his anguish. "When they saw him ... they could hardly recognize him; they began to weep aloud, and they tore their robes and sprinkled dust on their heads." They had heard it was bad, but nothing prepared them for this. Usually when you visit someone in bad condition, you try to cheer them up and tell them it's not so bad. Have you ever been so sick that when someone came to visit, they took one look at you and burst into tears? There's no use pretending.

The story continues: "Then they sat on the ground with him for seven days and seven nights. No one said a word to him, because they saw how great his suffering was."

It is worth pausing here for a moment. Imagine sitting with someone in silence for seven days. This was such a powerful act that it became part of Jewish life.

To this day the Jews will speak of sitting *shiva*—literally *"sitting sevens."* Friends will come and sit with one who mourns over a period of a week.

This incident with Job is perhaps the greatest example in Scripture of what Paul commands in Romans: "Mourn with those who mourn."

He doesn't say, "Find an explanation to give them about why they're suffering" or "Remind them everything is going to be okay, so they can stop crying now."

It is worth noting that after the seven days are over, Job's friends will speak—a lot. They will get into trouble for what they say. As with his wife, Job's friends have taken a lot of heat over the years, and for good reasons. Their words are not so hot.

But their silence was brilliant. Their silence was a gift.

Maybe the best way to mediate God's presence to someone who is suffering is to sit with them in silence.

Finally, after seven days, Job speaks. We wait to hear what he'll say. If he can just repeat what he says in chapter 1 — "God gives, God takes away, blessed be the name of the Lord" — the test will be over. It will be a short book.

"After this, Job opened his mouth and cursed the day of his birth."

This is the kind of thing that keeps Job off the motivational speaker circuit. I can guarantee you that Anthony Robbins or Charlie "Tremendous" Jones never say, "When your life is hard and torn, just curse the day when you were born."

Job goes on to request that that particular day be removed from the calendar. He requests "May those who curse days curse that day." (He doesn't tell us who "those who curse days" are; it seems like a limited profession.) For the next twenty-eight chapters Job pours out a level of bitterness, confusion, sorrow, and anger toward God that is staggering. He wants to know why God has forsaken him.

This is so raw that his friends can't stand it.

THE DOCTRINE OF RETRIBUTION

Job's friends spend twenty-two chapters voicing one central idea that was actually the primary theology of their day. It was written about in Mesopotamian wisdom literature. It is sometimes called "the doctrine of retribution." The idea is that goodness results in prosperity and blessing, wickedness results in suffering. Ironically, in their silence these friends drew Job closer to God. When they spoke, they pushed him away:

So Job, if you're suffering badly — you must have brought it on yourself. If you're no longer close to God — who do you think moved? If you will repent, he will deliver you from suffering.

Philip Yancey notes that the arguments voiced by Job's friends are being repeated in Christian churches today. Suffering people have told Yancey that those who make their suffering worse are Christians:

— "The reason you're in the hospital is spiritual warfare. If you were just engaging in spiritual warfare, Satan would be defeated and you'd be delivered."

— "God promises to heal—if we have enough faith. If you just had enough faith—just prayed boldly enough—you'd be healed."

We generally associate well-being with the presence of God and assume that suffering means someone has done something wrong. No one writes a book called *Where Is God When It Feels Good?* No one wins the lottery and cries out, "Why me, God?" And of course, it is true that pain was not part of God's original plan, and the day is coming when he will wipe every tear from every eye.

And yet …

While God hates pain, he can also redeem it. It does not mean he is absent. Years ago I helped conduct a survey that asked thousands of people what had most contributed to their spiritual growth. The number one answer was pain.

In summer I am tempted to think that because of my success, wealth, reputation, virtue, faith, I'm in control. My life will unfold how and when I want it to. In winter I learn I'm not running things after all. Somebody once said that the biggest difference between you and God is that God doesn't think he's you. In pain, we get very clear about not being God.

Of course, this doesn't mean we can go up to someone in enormous pain and say, "Well, this is good news because you're going to grow a lot!" Pain is deeper and more mysterious than that.

MINI-PAIN

One thing we can do is practice God's presence in moments of "mini-pain." Suppose I'm frustrated at standing in line at a 7-Eleven store. That's maybe a "one" on a pain scale of a thousand, but I can, in a sense, use it as a tool. I can ask God to be present with me in my frustration at having to wait. I can look for him in the presence of the clerk behind the counter who doesn't speak English very well. The practice of walking with God in mini-pain can serve people well when larger pain comes.

Almost six years ago I had the most painful year of my life (so far) when, for a variety of reasons, long-rooted patterns of living for other peoples' approval and applause came to the surface. The emptiness and hollowness of this life was so raw for me that every morning I woke up with a ball of pain in my stomach. I began to write to it in my journal each day: "Good morning, ball

> *While God hates pain, he can also redeem it. It does not mean he is absent.*

of pain, I wish you would go away...." Even though I have a Ph.D. in clinical psychology, I had never wanted to go through receiving counseling myself. I was the help-er, not the helpee. Pain changed all that. Now I *ran* for help.

Over time, although I never wanted to feel pain, I came to see that it was doing much good in me. I became much more aware of how everything meaningful in life rides on God. I became much more dependent on him. When people who knew me well would pause to lay hands on me and pray for me, it was like receiving life. Certain temptations involving success and achievement became much less seductive; spiritual reality got clearer.

The ball of pain gradually got smaller. It still revisits me from time to time. I never want it. But in a strange way I realize that it brings gifts from God that nothing else does.

I know, of course, that countless people have suffered infinitely more pain than I. And I don't believe God is the kind of person who delights in inflicting painful little moral object lessons on helpless mortals. But in my own life, at least, there is this strange duality about pain. It can cause me to wonder where God is, as nothing else can. And it can open me up to my dependence on his presence as nothing else can.

THE GIFT OF COMPLAINING

Job spends most of the book complaining to God. In the wintry books of the Bible, mostly people complain. There is a fascinating paradox in the book of Psalms. The Hebrew name for the psalms was *tehillim*—"praises."

Scholars sort out the psalms in different categories: psalms of thanksgiving; wisdom psalms, enthronement psalms. But by far the most common kind of psalm is called the lament—or complaint.

> You gave us up to be devoured like sheep
>> and have scattered us among the nations.
> You sold your people for a pittance,
>> gaining nothing from their sale....
> All this happened to us,
>> though we had not forgotten you
>> or been false to your covenant....

Israelites devoted more psalms to complaining than any other single category. This may be good news for you. Maybe you already know how to complain or would be willing to learn. Maybe complaining is your spiritual gift.

Old Testament scholar Ellen Davis has written that in the ancient world these complaint prayers are without parallel in other religions. In no other culture did people pray to their god in language that was so frank and even rude:

> You crushed us and made us a haunt for jackals....
> Awake, O Lord! Why do you sleep?
>> Rouse yourself! Do not reject us forever.
> Why do you hide your face
>> and forget our misery and oppression?...
> How long, O Lord, how long?

People of other ancient religions prayed. They made requests, offered worship, even cursed their enemies. Only Israel, in all the ancient world, prayed this kind of complaint prayers.

For good reason, because only Israel in all the ancient world believed that the great God who made the heavens and the earth cares that we are in pain and he can be expected to do something about it.

This is what makes these prayers so powerful—and an important part of our spiritual life. When we are passionately honest with God, when we are not indulging in self-pity or martyrdom but are genuinely opening ourselves up to God, when we complain in hope that God can still be trusted—then we are asking God to create the kind of condition in our heart that will make resting in his presence possible again. And God will come. But he may come in unexpected ways.

Lewis Smedes was a teacher of mine in seminary, one of the best writers and preachers I have ever known. Even though he was brilliant and accomplished and devoted to God, he suffered from a sense of inadequacy that at times grew into deep depression. At one point in his life he stopped preaching because he felt unqualified. God came to him through two avenues. One was a three-week experience of utter solitude, where he heard God promise to hold him up so vividly that, as he put it, he felt lifted from a black pit straight up into joy. The other avenue he describes this way:

> I have not been neurotically depressed since that day, though I must, to be honest, tell you that God also comes to me each morning and offers me a 20 milligram capsule of Prozac. He clears the garbage that accumulates in the canals of my brain overnight and gives me a chance to get a fresh morning start. I swallow every capsule with gratitude to God.

I love the picture Lew paints. I used to think that taking Prozac would be a sign of weak faith in God. But what if Prozac might be, not a substitute for God, but his gift? What if refusing might be spurning his hand because of pride? Maybe God is present in wise doctors and medication that makes synapses and neurotransmitters work right. Maybe weakness is really refusing—out of our own blindness and stubbornness—the help that God is offering.

THE KIND OF PERSON GOD IS

Job is quite convinced that God has left him, and he complains that what he really wants is a chance to square off with God mano-a-Dios.

"If only I knew where to find him;
    if only I could go to his dwelling!

I would state my case before him
    and fill my mouth with arguments."

Be careful what you ask for....

Toward the end of his story, Job gets his wish: "Then the Lord answered Job out of the storm."

What do you think that moment was like?

One of the most striking features of God's rebuttal in the book is that when he appears, he doesn't seem to get around to answering Job's question of *why*! He doesn't tell Job what the writer tells us—about the upper stage scenes of chapters 1–2.

God just asks him a bunch of questions Job can't answer. Why does God do this? At first glance it almost looks mean. And certainly part of what's happening is that God is pointing out Job has a finite mind and a limited point of view.

> *God's questions are filled with references to his extravagant goodness and provision even though there is no "strategic pain" in this.*

But there's something more. Ellen Davis writes that God's questions are indicating something about the kind of person he is. They are filled with references to God's extravagant goodness and provision even though there is no "strategic gain" in it at all.

"Who cuts a channel for the torrents of rain,...
    to water a land where no man lives,
        a desert with no one in it,
    to satisfy a desolate wasteland
        and make it sprout with grass?"

These lines would jump out at the reader in Job's day. Life in Israel depended on rainfall. They would never waste water. So why would God water "a land where no one lives"?

Because God is a God of gratuitous goodness. And he is uncontrollably generous. He is irrationally loving. He is good for no reason at all. He is good just because he loves to give. He sends streams of living water flowing out of sheer exuberant generosity. There is a wilderness where no one lives, yet it is full of beauty and grace because God makes a river run through it.

God delights in animals that are of no apparent use at all. The ostrich looks goofy and flaps her wings "joyfully" as if they could get her somewhere. She lays eggs and can't even remember where she left the babies. She doesn't seem to be worth much of an investment. But when she runs—oh my! "She laughs at horse and rider." Why would God waste such talent?

"I made the behemoth," God says—probably the hippopotamus. The creature is of no particular use: "Can anyone capture him when he is on the watch, With barbs can anyone pierce his nose?" The ancient world considered the hippo a chaotic monster that had to be destroyed—but not God. "He ranks first among the works of God." It's as if God is saying, "Best thing I ever did. I had my 'A' game going the day I made the behemoth."

God takes pleasure in wild oxen that will never plow; the wild donkey that will never be tamed; mountain goats that give birth in secret places man will never see; the leviathan that no one can catch. "Nothing on earth is his equal."

God creates, cares for, gives to, and delights in animals that don't appear to be good for anything. Why should God love a world like that? Anne Dillard writes, "Because the creator loves pizzazz." He revels in the beauty of the least strategic creature.

What God is really telling Job is, "I'm worth it. Life, following me—it's all worth it. Don't give up. This pain is not going to last forever. *I am the kind of God who is worth getting close to.*"

That is because God is gratuitously good—and uncontrollably generous—and irrationally loving. He just gives for no reason at all. It's his nature.

"God loves pizzazz." Maybe that's why we're here.

MADE TO CHARM HIM

My favorite author writes,

And when I begin to think about God's wild extravagance, his wastefulness, his passion for the unnecessary and the excessive and the completely useless, I am struck by a thought so wonderfully freeing I can do nothing but laugh. What if that extravagance extends to me? I am not a soldier for God, or a valued servant in the kingdom. I am a jester! I am the celestial equivalent of a peacock—a tiara—a talking doll. We were not made to serve God. We were made to charm him.

Job never does find out about the conversation in heaven. In that sense, his story is our story. On this earth we live on the lower stage. Winter comes, and we don't know why.

But Job finds out about something better. He finds out who God is.

"My ears had heard of you
but now my eyes have seen you."

That's enough.

God knows. God cares.

When God himself came to the earth, he came in winter. Jesus, like Job, was known as a "man of sorrows." He was acquainted with grief.

Where was God? He was on the ash heap. He, like Job, was so torn by suffering that no one recognized him: "We considered him stricken by God, smitten by him, and afflicted." He himself would go through the winter of the absence of God: "My God, my God, why have you forsaken me?"

On the cross is the ultimate paradox: God experiencing the absence of God so that he can draw close to us in our loss and grief and even in our God-forsakeness.

Nicholas Wolterstorff wrote a book called *Lament for a Son* when he entered into winter after his son died in an accident while mountain climbing. Wolterstorff writes of how we are told that no one can see the face of God and live. "I always thought that meant no one can see God's glory and live. A friend suggested that perhaps it means no one can see God's suffering and live. Or perhaps his suffering is his glory."

Never did we see his glory more clearly than when he was on the cross, taking our God-forsakeness on himself. Karl Barth wrote of the great miracle that God would rather be the suffering God of a suffering people than the blest God of an unblest people.

If it is winter in your life, and you wonder where God is, you don't have to wonder anymore. He is the God of the ash heap. Jesus was, in a sense, never closer to us than when he was farthest from the Father. Perhaps his suffering is his glory.

> *The cross is the ultimate paradox: God experiencing the absence of God so that he can draw close to us in our loss and grief.*

THE GLORY OF MAYBELLINE

Most of the last chapter in the book of Job is an epilogue. God tells Job's comforters, "I am angry with you ... because you have not spoken of me what is right, as my servant Job has."

(Imagine their amazement: Job complains about God; they stick up for God; they know they're right; then God shows up and says, "No, Job was right.")

God says that if Job will pray for them, he will forgive them.

We can guess that Job and his friends had a very interesting conversation. He prays. God forgives.

Then, in the final words the writer tells something we would tend to miss even though ancient readers would catch it. He tells us that Job had more children, then he gives names of Job's daughters, but not of his sons. In Hebrew genealogies that was unprecedented and unheard of. What's more, they are strange names. The subject of names in the Bible is worth a book on its own; they are vital expressions of human character and divine intent.

Usually Hebrew names are very serious; they express a character virtue or theological truth. But the names of Job's daughters are all about beauty. Jemima means "dove," considered a particularly lovely bird. The second daughter is named Keziah, which means "cinnamon," a prized spice. But the clincher is daughter number three: Keren-happuch, which means "horn of eye-shadow." Job named her after makeup. It's as if you named your daughter Estee Lauder or Maybelline.

Not only that, but Job gives them an inheritance. In the ancient, male-dominated world, a father with seven sons would never dream of leaving anything to a daughter. There might not be enough left over.

Sons were strategic. Sons were obligated to care for parents in their old age. Daughters were not strategic. Money that went to daughters would be used to care for their husbands' fathers; it was like putting money in somebody else's pension fund.

So why does the writer include this part of the story?

Because now Job delights in and gives to the least strategic creatures. Now he is gratuitously good. He is uncontrollably generous. He is irrationally loving. He gives for no reason at all.

Does this remind you of anybody?

Satan was dead wrong about old Job. The central question in Job is, can a human being hold on to God and faith and love even in the dead of winter?

One can. One did.

Job could not see the upper stage. Job did not know that his faithfulness had meaning beyond his wildest dreams. He did not know that something cosmic and eternal was at stake in his transitory life.

Sitting on an ash heap; scraping boils off his skin with shards of broken and discarded pots; feeling broken, sick, mocked, confused, and hopeless—Job discovered what people in pain sometimes learn better than anyone else. He was not alone after all.

Not even in winter.

CHAPTER 10

THE HEDGE

*Discernment is like driving an automobile at night; the head-
lights cast only enough light for us to see the next small bit of road
immediately in front of us. But that light is enough to take us home.*

Listening Hearts

We are living in temporary housing these days with a small backyard, and at the borderline of our yard is a hedge. It is growing
over a fence, so we cannot see or pass through to the other side. It has
become an obsession for Winston.

Winston is our Yorkshire terrier — not big enough to be a real
dog, more like a cat with delusions of dogness. Winston is on constant
patrol duty. He is sensitive to every creature that goes through our
property. He hears sounds and smells scents that are undetectable to
the rest of us. And Winston is convinced that there is Something on
the other side of the hedge.

When he is in the house, Winston will assume his scouting position on the headrest of a large chair in front of a window that over-
looks the backyard. His ears stand at attention; his head quivers like a
Bobble Head doll; his muscles go stiff as a marine's. When we let him
out back, he is frantic; he sniffs and barks and looks for an opening.

We don't know what it is. Maybe it's just rabbits and squirrels.
Maybe it's a giant, silent mastiff. Maybe it's a beautiful girl-dog pump-
ing out canine Love Potion #9.

All we know is that some sense or instinct or reflex has Winston in its grip and won't let go. The other side is his Holy of Holies; the hedge is a veil beyond which he may not pass. My wife, Nancy, is getting a little tired of it because when we bring him in, his front paws are caked with dirt—from trying to tunnel his way out of the backyard. Winston truly believes that there's Something on the other side of the hedge—and he wants to go over and see what it is.

I am living in temporary housing these days. My house gets a little grayer and more wrinkled every year, not-so-subtle reminders that sooner or later I will be evicted. Outside my door is a backyard called the Universe. And at the border of the universe is a hedge.

The hedge is a veil, a barrier that traps me in the aloneness of my backyard and cuts me off from some larger Presence. The hedge keeps me from seeing. The hedge is my finitude, my aloneness, my blindness, my sin.

Every day, millions of times a day, a heart stops beating, a pair of lungs stops breathing, and the hedge ceases to be their reality. If anyone could figure out a way to come back and give us a description of the other side, they could make a nice living. Some folks say they have gotten close enough to see a bright light, but they can offer no details. Others, like actress Shirley MacLaine, have claimed to go back and forth on a regular basis. The Afterlife is a hub city for their souls the way Atlanta is for Delta Airlines, yet they never bring back substantial evidence like a postcard or a souvenir.

Some people are convinced that there is Nothing behind the hedge, that our backyard is all there is, that what you see is what you get. But the whispers and rumors of the Presence are curiously stubborn. There seems to be in the human race an irrepressible instinct that Something lies behind the hedge, that there is more to existence than a swirl of molecules and atoms, that death is a gate and not a fence, that reality is bigger than just our backyard. So people keep poking and digging around the backyard—building pyramids and painting chapel ceilings—and getting their paws muddy and saying prayers to Someone behind the hedge.

THIN PLACES

Philip Yancey writes that "Celtic spirituality speaks of 'thin places' where the natural and supernatural worlds come together at their narrowest." The birth of a child, the words to an ancient hymn, the sight of the sun rising over the rim of a sleeping world—the thin places can be as momentous as life and death or as tiny as a hummingbird. For some people the veil seems to be thinner than others—a hairbreadth, like the space between Adam and God in the Sistine Chapel.

Proof is hard to come by—at least if you want to stay in the backyard. Death will bring the ultimate answer, but once it does, you won't be able to tell anyone.

It is a great irony to me that the keenest minds in the world spend their lives thinking and probing and studying to answer this one question and never know for sure, yet the biggest fool in the universe knows one second after he dies. You find out for sure—or there's no you anymore to find out anything—one second after it's too late to do anything about it. I almost always have this thought when I hear of someone who has died: *Now he knows.* During the week I write this, those someones are a former president named Ronald Reagan and a singer named Ray Charles and a fifteen-year-old boy from our church. And now they know.

Those who believe that Something lies behind the hedge must struggle with why the hedge is there at all. Why does the Something stay so hidden? Does the hedge serve a purpose? Is it possible that there is some good in not knowing?

Those who believe that Nothing lies behind the hedge must struggle with why the rumors of Something are so persistent. Harder still, they must struggle with what to do during our brief time in the backyard if the backyard turns out to be nothing more than a cemetery.

This much is certain: Every human being has lived in temporary housing. Every one of them has waited for their turn to leave the backyard.

Until one day....

Until a man who looked like all other men made a breathtaking claim. He said he came from the other side of the hedge. He said no one has to be alone anymore. No one has to live in fear. He said a new kind of life — life with-God — is now available to anyone who wants it. And he didn't bring this life just to give us comfort. He brought it to give us a mission. He said anyone who enters this life will join him in becoming carriers of it to others in the backyard.

THE HEDGE-BREAKER

Jesus came as the Hedge-Breaker.

I believe there has been a fundamental misunderstanding about Jesus' message in our day. People have gotten the idea that Jesus' gospel — his Good News — is primarily about how to get ready for life on the other side of the hedge, rather than the announcement that the mysterious Someone has broken through the hedge and entered our own backyard. This misunderstanding has had the devastating consequence of keeping many people from seeking to experience God's presence in their lives here and now.

A fundamental misunderstanding is keeping many people from seeking to experience God's presence in their lives here and now.

Karen Mains writes about a Sunday school teacher who wondered if her class understood the gospel, so she asked them:

If I sold my house and car, had a big garage sale, and gave all my money to the church, would that get me into heaven?

No!

If I cleaned the church every day, mowed the yard, and kept everything neat and tidy, would that get me into heaven?

No!

Well, if I was kind to animals and gave candy to all the children and loved my husband, would that get me into heaven?

No!

Well, then, how can I get into heaven?

A five-year-old boy shouted out, "You gotta be dead!"

Here is the difficulty: If you gotta be dead, then the gospel doesn't have much to do with today. However, when we look closely at what

Jesus calls his good news, he does not put it in terms of something that happens after you die. He speaks of something that happens on *this* side of the hedge.

The good news Jesus announced was simply this: God has invaded our backyard and is making his presence and power available to anybody who wants him. Right here. Right now. "The time has come," Jesus says. Now God is closer than you think.

The tragic truth is that many people have exchanged Jesus' "Gospel of Life-with-God Here and Now" for a gospel that doesn't kick in until later: *You gotta be dead.*

A scene in a certain film expresses the way many people think of the gospel. In *Monty Python and the Holy Grail*, King Arthur and his knights have to get across a bridge to complete their quest. The bridge is guarded by an old man who tells them they each must answer three questions in order to cross; if they get one answer wrong, they are plunged into the abyss.

The first knight steps up. "State your name" (he does). "State your quest" (he does). "What's your favorite color?" ("Red.") He crosses the bridge, amazed it was so easy.

Second knight's turn. He is asked to state his name and quest, but his third question is, "What's the capital of Assyria?" "I don't know that—ahhhhhh!" He is thrown into the abyss.

The third knight is terrified. He correctly gives his name and quest, but when asked the third question ("What's your favorite color?"), he is so nervous that he responds, "Red—no, blue—ahhhhh!" Abyss.

Now it is King Arthur's turn. Same drill on the first two questions; the third one makes for a running gag throughout the film: "What is the air-speed velocity of a coconut-laden swallow?" Arthur responds with the standard reply throughout the movie: "That depends—is it an African or European swallow?"

"*I* don't know that—ahhhhhh!" and the *bridgekeeper* is cast into the abyss.

Many people have reduced the gospel to this: When you die, there will be a bridge to the other side. The gospel is the correct answer to the question that will mean they have to let you cross. If you don't know the right answer, you get cast down into the Abyss. The gospel is thought to be the secret password that gets me through the hedge.

The problem is, where in the New Testament does Jesus say, "Now I'm going to give you the minimal requirements you have to meet so that you can get into heaven when you die"?

He doesn't. Jesus' gospel includes forgiveness of our sins as a gift of grace. It includes the promise that death will not have the last word, that our eternal life with God will never cease.

But it includes more than that. As we saw in chapter 1, the promise fulfilled in Jesus' coming is the unifying theme of Scripture: Immanuel, "God with us." Jesus said, "Anyone who loves me will obey my teaching. My Father will love them, and we will come to them and *make our home with them.*"

JACOB'S LADDER REVISITED

Remember Jacob's dream at Beth-el, which we talked about in chapter 1? He had a vision of a ladder that stood on the earth while the top of it reached to heaven, and the angels climbed up and down on it; it was a vision of a "with-God" life here on earth. At the beginning of his ministry Jesus explained his mission to a man named Nathanael: "I tell you the truth, you shall see heaven open, and the angels of God ascending and descending on the Son of Man."

Jesus is referring, of course, to Jacob's vision. What Jacob dreamed of was now a reality to anyone who wanted it. Jesus himself came as "Jacob's ladder" that now reaches down to your life and mine.

Jesus' overall mission was to bring the reality of God's presence and power over to our side of the hedge.

Many people think the only real reason Jesus came to earth was to die on the cross. But death on the cross was just one part of his mission. His overall mission was to bring the reality of God's presence and power over to our side of the hedge.

Things in our backyard are not going so well. As I am writing this, a newspaper has a story about nation-sponsored kidnapping in Zambia—with torture, amputation, genocide, and heart-wrenching pictures of mass graves. There is also a story of the mother of a three-year-old son and a two-year-old daughter who strapped a bomb to her body, killing herself and four other people, because "it was always my wish to turn my body into deadly shrapnel and to knock on the door of heaven with the skulls of my enemies."

I was at a meeting with the Christian activist Jim Wallis, who told me that every day, 30,000 children die of preventable causes. Every day. Sometimes our backyard looks like a cemetery.

MAKE UP THERE COME DOWN HERE

Not only did Jesus come as the Hedge-Breaker, but he told his followers that they were to devote their lives to his project. In his most famous prayer he said we are to pray,

> "Our Father in heaven,
> hallowed be your name.
> your kingdom come,
> your will be done
>   on earth as it is in heaven."

Sometimes people pray a version of the *Star Trek* prayer to Scottie: "Beam me up." Many people think our job is to get my afterlife destination taken care of, then tread water till we all get ejected and God comes back and torches this place. But Jesus never told anybody—neither his disciples nor us—to pray, "Get me out of here so I can go up there." His prayer was, "Make up there come down here." Make things down here run the way they do up there.

Jesus told us to pray, "Bring heaven down here." We begin with our body, our mind, our appetites. Then it spreads to the office, our family, our neighborhood, our church, our country.

God doesn't reveal himself to us just to make us happy or to deliver us from loneliness. He also comes to us so that we can in turn be conduits of his presence to other people. He invites us to join him in making things down here the way they are up there.

This news is the best news the human race has ever heard. It is not just good news for the world around us; it is good news for us. Psychologist Viktor Frankl wrote, "What man actually needs is not a tension-less state but rather the striving and struggling for some goal worthy of him. What he needs is not the discharge of tension at any cost, but the call of a potential meaning waiting to be fulfilled by him."

This is maybe the most dangerous, exciting, life-altering prayer a human being can pray: "God, make up there come down here." Every time you pray it, your life becomes Beth-el, the place where God dwells, and the "with-God" life breaks through the hedge.

A PLACE TO START

Start by asking yourself this question: "Where do I want to see God's presence and power break into my world? Where would I especially like God to use me to make things down here run the way they do up there?"

Jesus didn't just come to pierce the hedge that separates God from human beings. He came to tear down the hedges of fear and suspicion and bitterness that separate human beings from each other. In Paul's day, the big hedge was the one that separated Jewish people from Gentiles. But Jesus, Paul said, "made the two one, and has destroyed the barrier, the dividing wall of hostility.... through him we both have access to the Father by one Spirit."

"God, make up there come down here." Three women from the church I serve prayed this prayer one day. They were on a women's retreat, but they were playing hooky from a session that was being taught by my wife, and they started dreaming together about being "kingdom-bringers." Eventually they came to one of our pastors, called "J.D.," and told him about their dreams.

"What do you want to do?" he asked. They told him they wanted to save all the babies in Africa.

J. D. told them that was kind of big for a starter project, so would they be willing to begin by trying to spend a day helping out an under-resourced school?

So the women started to pray: "God, make up there come down here for this little school in East Palo Alto." In our area, one of the big hedges is the Route 101 freeway that separates East Palo Alto from Palo Alto. Palo Alto is the home of Stanford University and Silicon Valley; it was listed recently in *Forbes* magazine as the number one area in the world to live in if you want to get rich. East Palo Alto is an under-resourced community right next door; a few years ago it led the nation in murders per capita.

This group of women schemed and prayed and planned and came up with a challenge: How about having one thousand people from our church give up a day to plant trees and tile floors and paint murals at this school?

I didn't think there was any way we could get a thousand people to do this, but I said I would announce it and see what happens. We ended up having to cut off sign-ups at twelve hundred people because we couldn't handle any more volunteers. The best part was watching God present and at work in ways none of us could have planned.

A young coed was visiting our church from college and heard about this plan. Not only did she want to come, but when she went back to school and told her sorority, they wanted to come too. So we ended up with over a thousand people from our church—and thirty sorority sisters. This meant that scores of single young males suddenly felt God prompting them to serve also.

Some people were talking to an East Palo Alto city official about this at a Starbucks, and he told the store manager, "You ought to donate enough coffee for all these people on Saturday morning."

And the Starbucks guy said, "Okay."

The city official decided to go for broke: "You ought to deliver it too."

And the Starbucks guy said, "Okay."

The three women went to Home Depot. They had no titles or credentials, just a conviction that God would help them bring up there to down here. They told the Home Depot guy what they were up to, and then said: "We need $10,000 worth of equipment. We don't have any money for this—you ought to just donate it."

And the Home Depot guy said, "Okay."

So they got $10,000 worth of material free.

They were talking to a woman who doesn't attend the church. By now you can fill in the conversational details by yourself: the school ended up getting $20,000 worth of playground material for free.

For a whole day there was music blaring and balloons flying and five-year-olds serving next to eighty-five-year-olds and people working together from churches of every stripe and ethnicity. It was the single most joyous day I have seen a church have. Those of us who served were blessed far beyond those we offered services to. And it was because of a single prayer: "Help us make up there come down here."

These three women have actually adopted a mission statement for their friendship that leaves the mission statements I have seen for most churches and corporations all behind: "To identify our neighbors' greatest needs, and surprise our church into hilarious giving by providing impact-full, totally happenin' and celebratory opportunities to serve."

GOD AT THE DMV

Where do you experience an authentic level of passion about things down here not running the way they are up there? Maybe it happens when you look at people who suffer from poverty or illiteracy or abuse in families. Maybe you find your heart stirred when you come into contact with people who have deep emotional hurts or children who have no homes or marriages that are falling apart.

> *Where do you experience an authentic level of passion about things down here not running the way they are up there?*

Internally, most of us want to experience the *feelings* of God's presence; a deeper sense of peace and assurance, a stronger surge of joy, a clearer word of guidance. Is it even possible for the practice of the presence of God to become a thinly veiled pursuit of emotional comfort? But ironically, none of these feelings are strictly necessary for us to become *agents* of God's presence for other people. All that is necessary is a single intent: "Lord, where do you want to use me to help things down here run the way they do up there?"

It doesn't always happen in dramatic or visible ways.

There is no place where God's presence cannot break into you. I was in the Department of Motor Vehicles two weeks ago. David asked once, "Where can I go from your Spirit? Where can I flee from your presence?" If I had to take a stab at that one, I'd guess the DMV.

I was standing in line, resenting the glacial-like pace at which everything was moving (or rather, not moving), caught up in how *my* little kingdom was being inconvenienced. The elderly woman in front of me was taking forever. Then the prayer came to me: "God, make things down here like they are up there." And the thought occurred to me, *I could go over and see if I can help that woman.* It turned out she was all alone and extremely anxious and having a hard time communicating with the man behind the desk, who could not speak English well. I spent perhaps five minutes with her. It was a tiny kindness; someone less preoccupied than I wouldn't have required a divine push at all. But for a few moments I got to help the kingdom of love be present to someone who needed it. For a few moments, the kingdom broke into the DMV.

For you, this breakthrough means starting with the relationships closest to you: "Let your kingdom come into my friendships, my family, my marriage." Not long ago Nancy and I were having dinner with another couple. She and I had an interaction during the course of the conversation that I just didn't like.

Later that night, when we were alone, I was thinking about that interaction. I could still feel some anger. I had this direct thought: Talk to Nancy about it.

I had a few choices. First, I could nurse a silent grudge. I know how to do this; I'm Swedish, so it's in my genes. Second, I could talk about it in a way to put her on the defensive. I talk a lot—I talk for a living—so I know how to do that.

But the thought came to me: Tell her clearly: Here's what happened, here's what I didn't like, here's why it's a vulnerable subject to me, here's what I'd like you to think about.

So that's what I did. We had a brief talk.

A few minutes later Nancy came back to me: "I just want to tell you, when you told me about that, it communicated to me that you really care about us and our relationship. It made me feel closer to you."

She said, "I thought it was sexy."

(I'm not making this up. And I have her permission to include this here.)

I told her about something she did that I didn't like—and not only did she not withdraw, she said that she thought my honesty was sexy.

I started trying to think of other things she does that I don't like. Getting that kind of response, I was ready to start making stuff up.

GOD'S COSTLY PRESENCE

Sometimes offering yourself as a vessel for the presence and work of God is costly. Richard Felix has recently written one of the most moving books I have read in a long time, *The School of Dying Graces*. He writes of his wife's long, terminal struggle with breast cancer. She endured all the tortures that might promise healing: a lumpectomy, three rounds of chemotherapy, a double mastectomy, radiation of the lungs and brain, a bone marrow transplant, a miracle drug, and experimental therapies.

Sometimes offering yourself as a vessel for the presence and work of God is costly.

After almost two years of this agony, her oncologist told her that the Beast (which is what Vivian called her cancer) would win. She could expect to live four to six more weeks.

Vivian and Richard went to their favorite ocean-view restaurant, which had been the setting for so much of their life together and now would be the setting for the beginning of the end. She told him she needed to prepare to die. She asked if he would take responsibility for praying for a miracle, so that she could turn her focus away from the disease and onto the presence of God.

"I plan to enroll," she told him, "in the school of dying graces."

Richard writes of how difficult it was to see her enter "her personal Gethsemane, a place of great suffering that became holy ground for her most intimate encounters with God. I could not follow her there, though I longed to do so with every cell in my body." Yet, in a way, in choosing to take her suffering on himself, he *did* enter his own Gethsemane. He entered into the highest kind of love, the love that Jesus suffered, the love that embraces suffering for the sake of the beloved.

One June day in the year 2000, Vivian Felix's battle with cancer ended. *And now she knows.*

"God, make up there come down here." This was essentially Richard's prayer. It did not get answered in the way he wanted. The full healing of heaven did not descend to Vivian's body. But in their love for each other, in their prayerfully embraced suffering *for* each other, there was an expression of love that no cancer could ever defeat. And in the love he gave them, God made down here a little more like up there.

God, make up there come down here.

It can happen. Every time you are in conflict with someone, want to hurt them, gossip about them, or avoid them, but instead go to them and seek reconciliation and forgiveness —

The kingdom is breaking into this world.

Every time you have a chunk of money and decide to give sacrificially to somebody who is hungry or homeless or poor —

The kingdom is breaking into the world.

Anytime someone has an addiction and wants to partner with God so much that they're willing to stop hiding, acknowledge the truth, and get help from a loving community —

The kingdom is breaking into the world.

Every time a workaholic parent decides to stop idolizing their job, rearranges their life to begin to love and care for the little children entrusted to them —

The kingdom is breaking into the world.

Every time you love, every time you include someone who's lonely, every time you encourage someone who's defeated, every time you

challenge somebody who's wandering off the path, every time you
serve the under-resourced—

It is a *sign* that the kingdom is once more breaking into the world.

When Jesus entered humanity, when the baby was laid in the
manger, the kingdom of God had a tiny little beachhead in this world.
He formed a little community; and when he left, there was a toehold
in Jerusalem. Then it started to spread—to Judea, to Samaria, to Athens, to Rome. To every country. From ancient cathedrals in England
to underground house churches in China to storefront churches in
inner-city Detroit.

One day a little beachhead got formed in your life. It doesn't matter whether your life seems messy to you. It doesn't matter if you don't
fully understand how the kingdom works. Someone has come from
the other side of the hedge. And he uses you and me. He lives in our
backyard now.

SCRIPTURE VERSIONS

Scripture quotations marked KJV are taken from the King James Version.

Scripture quotations marked NIV® are taken from the *Holy Bible, New International Version®*. Copyright © 1973, 1978, 1984 by International Bible Society. Used by permission of Zondervan. All rights reserved.

Scripture quotations marked TNIV® are taken from the *Holy Bible, Today's New International Version®*. Copyright © 2002, 2004 by International Bible Society. Used by permission of Zondervan. All rights reserved.

Scripture quotations marked NRSV are taken from the *New Revised Standard Version of the Bible,* copyright 1989, Division of Christian Education of the National Council of the Churches of Christ in the United States of America. Used by permission. All rights reserved.

Scripture quotations marked NASB are taken from the *New American Standard Bible,* Copyright © 1960, 1962, 1963, 1968, 1971, 1972, 1973, 1975, 1977 by The Lockman Foundation. Used by permission.

SOURCES

CHAPTER 1: GOD'S GREAT DESIRE

11: Thomas Kelly, *A Testament of Devotion*. San Francisco: HarperSan-Francisco, 1992, 90.

11: *Psycho*: Film directed by Alfred Hitchcock in 1960, based on the novel *Psycho* by Robert Bloch, 1959.

12: "All of man's potential": Sandra L. Bertman, *Art Annotations*, from the Literature, Arts, and Medicine Database at http:// endeavor.med.nyu. edu/lit-med/.

12: "I have my beard": Massio Giacometti, ed., *The Sistine Chapel*. New York: Harmony Books, 1986, 234.

13: "I am no painter": Quoted in Lewis Smedes, *Standing on the Promises*. Nashville: Thomas Nelson, 1998, 28.

13: "This is my Father's world": Maltbie D. Babcock (1858–1901).

13: "The heavens are telling": Psalm 19:1–2 NRSV.

13: Garrison Keillor: Quoted in David Myers, *The Pursuit of Happiness*. New York: Avon Books, 1992, 45.

15: "Do not be terrified": Joshua 1:9 NIV.

15: "Yea, though I walk": Psalm 23:4 KJV.

15: "I am *with you* always": Matthew 28:20 NASB.

15: "God's dwelling place": Revelation 21:3 TNIV.

15: Dallas Willard and Richard Foster, unpublished manuscript.

16: "Find a place": Quoted in Suzanne Farnham et al., *Listening Hearts: Discerning Call in Community*. Harrisburg, PA: Morehouse Publishing, 1991, 1.

16: Sofia Cavalletti, *The Religious Potential of the Child: 6 to 12 Years Old*. Chicago: Liturgy Training Publications, 2002.

16: Anne Lamott: From an address heard by the author.

17: Dallas Willard, *Hearing God*. Downers Grove, IL: InterVarsity Press, 1999, 186.

17: "The LORD bless you": Numbers 6:24–25 NRSV.

17: "A certain place": Genesis 28:11 NIV. This story about Jacob is told in verses 10–22.

18: "Resting on the earth": Genesis 28:12 NIV.

18: "I am the LORD": Genesis 28:13, 15 NIV.

18: "When Jacob awoke": Genesis 28:16–17 NIV.

18: God would later reveal himself: Genesis 32:22–32.

18: "Wake up, O sleeper": Ephesians 5:14 NIV.

19: "But Esau ran to meet Jacob": Genesis 33:4 NIV.

19: "To see your face": Genesis 33:10 NIV.

20: "I have been asked by some": Mallory Ortberg, unpublished manuscript.

20: "Those who are with us": 2 Kings 6:16 NIV. This story about Elisha is told in 2 Kings 6:8–23.

20: The story about Samuel and Eli is told in 1-Samuel 3.

21: "Didn't our hearts burn": Luke 24:32 paraphrased.

21: Frederick Buechner, *Listening to Your Life*. San Francisco: HarperSanFrancisco, 1992, 2.

21: Thomas à Kempis, *The Imitation of Christ*. Notre Dame, IN: Ave Maria Press, 1989, 61.

21: Jean Pierre de Caussade, *The Sacrament of the Present Moment*. Translated by Kitty Muggeridge. San Francisco: Harper & Row, 1982, 68.

22: "The good brother found God": Brother Lawrence, *The Practice of the Presence of God*. Springdale, PA: Whitaker House, 1982, 90.

23: "The most holy and necessary practice": Ibid., 61.

26: "God alone is capable": Ibid., 87.

CHAPTER 2: WHERE'S WALDO?

27: Armand Nicholi, *The Question of God*. Quoted in Karen Mains, *The God Hunt*. Downers Grove, IL: InterVarsity Press, 2003, 13.

28: "Be aware of what's": www.candlewick.com/cwp/authill.asp?b=Author&m=bio&id=1784&pix=n. Accessed September 7, 2004. The Where's Waldo books are published in the United States by Candlewick Press.

29: Brother Lawrence, *The Practice of the Presence of God*. Springdale, PA: Whitaker House, 1982, 51.

29: "The LORD saw how great": Genesis 6:5–6 NIV.

29: "I will make a covenant" (Noah): See Genesis 9:8–17.

30: "I will make a covenant" (Abraham): See Genesis 17:1–14.

31: "Summertime, and the livin'": Lyrics by DuBose Heyward from the folk opera *Porgy and Bess*.

31: "There is the sea": Psalm 104:25–26 NIV.

32: St. John of the Cross, *Dark Night of the Soul*. Translated by E. Allison Peers. New York: Dover, 2003.

33: "In those days, the word": 1 Samuel 3:1 NIV.

34: "I hold this against you": Revelation 2:4 NIV.

35: Pat Conroy, *Prince of Tides*. Boston: Houghton Mifflin, 1986, 277–78, italics mine.

35: William Barry, *Finding God in All Things*. Notre Dame, IN: Ave Maria Press, 1991, 14–15.

36: Bob Fisher, "The Case for Film Dailies," *American Cinematographer* (April 2004): 90ff.

37: Dallas Willard, *The Renovation of the Heart*. Colorado Springs: NavPress, 2002, 43.

37: "Where are you?": Genesis 3:9–10 NIV.

38: "But he did not know": Judges 16:20 NIV.

40: George MacDonald, *Thomas Wingfold, Curate*. Eureka, CA: Sunrise Publishers, 1988, 430.

41: "You can walk by faith": See 2 Corinthians 5:7.

42: Thomas Merton: Cited in Philip Yancey, *Reaching for the Invisible God*. Grand Rapids: Zondervan, 2000, 27.

42: Brother Lawrence, *Practicing the Presence of God*, 40.

42: Meister Eckhart: Quoted in Belden C. Lane, "A Hidden and Playful God," in *Christian Century* (September 30, 1987): 812.

43: "Majesty": Isaiah 53:2 NIV.

43: "Despised and rejected": Isaiah 53:3 NIV.

CHAPTER 3: LIFE WITH GOD

45: J. D. Salinger, *Franny and Zooey*. New York: Bantam Books, 1964, 170.

46: "The one thing needful": The story of Mary and Martha is in Luke 10:38–42.

46: Socrates: Quoted in Plato's *Apology* 38a.

47: "Wicked and lazy": Matthew 25:26 NRSV.

47: "Go and work in the vineyard": Matthew 21:28 NRSV.

48: "My food is to do": See John 4:34 NIV.

48: Send workers into the field: See Luke 10:2.

48: Go throughout the world: See Matthew 28:18–20.

49: "I am a Jew": Acts 22:3 NRSV.

49: Ancient Talmud story: Told in Benjamen Blech, *The Complete Idiot's Guide to Understanding Judaism*. Indianapolis: Alpha Books, 1999, 259.

49: "Let your house be": From the Mishnah, quoted in Marvin Wilson, *Our Father Abraham: Jewish Roots of the Christian Faith*. Grand Rapids: Eerdmans, 1999, 300.

50: Ray van der Laan: From a sermon preached at Willow Creek Community Church in South Barrington, Illinois, in July 2003.

53: "Simon, Simon": Luke 22:31 NIV.

53: "Saul, Saul": Acts 9:4 TNIV.

58: Dallas Willard, *Renovation of the Heart*. Colorado Springs: NavPress, 2002, 70.

59: Brother Lawrence, *Practicing the Presence of God*. Springdale, PA: Whitaker House, 1982, 36.

59: "Wants to go faster": Ibid., 45.

59: "It is not necessary": Ibid., 81.

CHAPTER 4: THE GREATEST MOMENT OF YOUR LIFE

61: William Blake, "Auguries of Innocence."

62: "This is the day": Psalm 118:24 NIV.

62: "They are new": Lamentations 3:23 NIV.

62: "Be very careful": Ephesians 5:15–16 TNIV.

63: Jean Pierre de Caussade, *The Sacrament of the Present Moment*. Translated by Kitty Muggeridge. San Francisco: Harper & Row, 1982, 27.

63: Frederick Buechner, *The Alphabet of Grace*. New York: Harper & Row, 1970, 12.

64: "The Nile will teem": Exodus 8:2–3 NIV. The story of the plague of frogs is told in Exodus 8:1–15.

64: Ken Davis, *Lighten Up*. Grand Rapids: Zondervan, 2000, 55.

65: Davis: Ibid.

65: David Pears, *Motivated Irrationality*. South Bend, IN: St. Augustine's Press, 1997.

66: "Today, if you hear his voice": Hebrews 3:7–8, 13 TNIV.

67: Abraham Heschel, *The Sabbath: Its Meaning for Modern Man*. Boston: Shambhala, 2003, 14.

67: "And there was evening": Genesis 1:5 NIV.

67: Eugene Peterson: From an address heard by the author.

67: "In vain you rise early": Psalm 127:2 NIV.

68: Asleep in Gethsemane: See Matthew 26:36–46.

68: Asleep in the boat: See Mark 4:35–41.

68: Brother Lawrence, *Practicing the Presence of God*. Springdale, PA: Whitaker House, 1982, 31.

68: "Be angry but": Ephesians 4:26–27 NRSV.

69: Frank Laubach, *Letters by a Modern Mystic*. Old Tappan, NJ: Revell, 1958, 205.

69: "In the morning I": Psalm 5:3 NIV.

70: Dietrich Bonhoeffer, *Life Together*. Minneapolis: Augsburg Press, 1996, 99.

70: "Cleanse me with hyssop": Psalm 51:7 NIV.

70: Their daily bread: See the Lord's Prayer, as in Matthew 6:9, 11.

71: "Food from the earth": Psalm 104:14–15 NRSV.

71: "Eat your bread": Ecclesiastes 9:7, various versions of the Bible.

71: Those with whom he ate: Luke 15:1–2.

71: Robert Putnam, *Bowling Alone: The Collapse and Revival of American Community*. New York: Simon & Schuster, 2001, 100–101.

71: "Blessed art Thou, O God": Quoted in a message at Willow Creek given by Ray Vander Laan entitled "The Dust of the Rabbi."

71: "Not live on bread": Matthew 4:4 NIV.

71: Nothing can separate us: See Romans 8:38–39.

72: I can do all things: Philippians 4:13.

72: God is light: 1-John 1:5.

73: Bonhoeffer, *Life Together*, 99.

74: Bartimaeus: Mark 10:46–52.

74: A woman with chronic illness: Mark 5:21–35.

74: A leper: Matthew 8:1–4; Mark 1:40–45.

74: Sinful woman: Luke 7:36–50.

CHAPTER 5: A BEAUTIFUL MIND

77: Frank Laubach, *Letters by a Modern Mystic*. Old Tappan, NJ: Revell, 1958.

77: *A Beautiful Mind*: Film directed by Ron Howard in 2001, based on the book *A Beautiful Mind* by Sylvia Nasar. New York: Simon & Schuster, 2001.

79: "Always before me": See Psalm 16:8.

79: "His sheep follow him": John 10:4–5 TNIV.

79: "The word is very near you": Deuteronomy 30:14 NIV.

79: Thomas Kelly, *A Testament of Devotion.* San Francisco: HarperSan-Francisco, 1992, 92ff.

81: The wind blows: John 3:8.

82: In one experiment: Cited in David Myers, *The Pursuit of Happiness.* New York: Avon Books, 1992, 66.

83: "The mind controlled": Romans 8:6 TNIV.

84: John Calvin, *Institutes of the Christian Religion,* book I, ch. 13, sect. 1. Translated by Henry Beveridge. Grand Rapids: Eerdmans, 1990.

85: Mihalyi Csikszentmihalyi, *Flow: The Psychology of Optimal Experience.* New York: HarperCollins, 1990, 119.

86: "Futility of their thinking": Ephesians 4:17 TNIV.

86: "Gave them over": Romans 1:28 NIV.

86: "Be transformed": Romans 12:2 NRSV.

86: "Not given us the spirit": 2 Timothy 1:7 KJV.

87: Psalm 10:4 TNIV.

88: Double-mindedness: James 1:8.

88: *Yetzer hara*: Tilden Edwards, *Living in the Presence.* New York: HarperCollins, 1987, 9.

88: Lukewarmness: Revelation 3:16.

88: Fruit of the Spirit: Galatians 5:22–23.

88: "The LORD is my Shepherd": Psalm 23:1, various versions of the Bible.

89: Laubach, *Letters from a Modern Mystic,* 7.

89: "Finally, brothers and sisters": Philippians 4:8 TNIV.

90: "We take every thought": 2 Corinthians 10:5 NRSV.

92: "Speak, LORD, for your servant": 1 Samuel 3:9, various versions of the Bible.

92: Isaac: Genesis 24:63 NIV.

92: "Delight is in the law": Psalm 1:2 NIV.

92: "Not let this Book": Joshua 1:8 NIV.

92: Psalm 16:8 NIV.

93: "He who began a good work": See Philippians 1:6.

CHAPTER 6: WALDO JUNIOR

95: Brother Lawrence, *Practicing the Presence of God.* Springdale, PA: Whitaker House, 1982, 93.

95: Esther de Waal, *Seeking God: The Way of St. Benedict.* Collegeville, MN: Liturgical Press, 1984, 126.

95: "Oh, that you would": Isaiah 64:1 NIV.

95: Father Damien: For more on Father Damien, see various books or, for example, the website for Kalaupapa National Historical Park at www. nps.gov./kala/docs/damien.htm.

96: "Where two or three": Matthew 18:20 KJV.

96: "Whatever you did": Matthew 25:40 NIV.

96: "Whoever is kind": Proverbs 19:17 NRSV.

97: "No one has ever seen": 1 John 4:12 TNIV.

97: Saul: See Acts 9:1–9.

97: C. S. Lewis, *The Screwtape Letters.* Reprint: New York: HarperCollins, 2001, 6.

98: "Thou art the man!": 2 Samuel 12:7 KJV.

98: "Who knows but that": Esther 4:14 NIV.

98: Joseph and Mary: Luke 2:22–35.

98: Moses' father-in-law: Exodus 18:13–26.

98: "A great man": 2 Kings 5:1, various versions of the Bible. The story of Naaman is told in 2 Kings 5.

99: "A man's gotta know": The catch phrase of the character played by Clint Eastwood in the film *Magnum Force* (Warner Studios, 1973).

102: John Woolman: See, for example, *The Journal of John Woolman* (with an Appreciation and Notes by John G. Whittier). London: Andrew Melrose, 1898.

103: Henry Cloud and John Townsend, *How People Grow.* Grand Rapids: Zondervan, 2001, 119–20.

103: Pico della Mirandola, *Oration on the Dignity of Man* (1486).

103: "Manifestations of human dignity": Massio Giacometti, ed., *The Sistine Chapel.* New York: Harmony Books, 1986, 126.

104: "God in his grace": Ibid., 124.

104: "Jesus frequently": Suzanne Farnham et al., *Listening Hearts: Discerning Call in Community.* Harrisburg, PA: Morehouse Publishing, 1991, 44.

105: Parable about sheep and goats: Matthew 25:31–46.

105 : Frank Laubach, *Man of Prayer.* Syracuse, NY: Laubach Literacy International, 1990, 329–30.

107: "Love your enemies": Matthew 5:44 NIV.

107: "Whatever you did": Matthew 25:40 NIV.

107: "Where two or three": Matthew 18:20 KJV.

CHAPTER 7: SPIRITUAL PATHWAYS

109: C. S. Lewis, *The Problem of Pain.* Reprint: New York: HarperCollins, 2001, 154.

111: "The Lord God made them all": From the hymn "All Things Bright and Beautiful" by Cecil F. Alexander (1848).

111: Gary Thomas, *Sacred Pathways*. Grand Rapids: Zondervan, 2000, 14.

112: "With all your heart": Deuteronomy 6:5 NIV.

112: "With all your mind": Luke 10:27 TNIV.

113: "Now to him who": Ephesians 3:20–21 TNIV.

113: "Knowledge puffs up": 1 Corinthians 8:1 NIV.

113: "Where two or three": Matthew 18:20 KJV.

113: Robert Wuthnow, *Sharing the Journey: Support Groups and the Quest for a New Community*. New York: Free Press, 1996.

114: Peter and legalists: See Galatians 2:11–21.

115: "Whatever you did for the least": Matthew 25:40.

115: Dorcas: See Acts 9:36.

116: "I rejoiced with those": Psalm 122:1 NIV.

116: "When I tried to understand": Psalm 73:16–17 NIV.

117: Danced before the Lord: See 2 Samuel 6:12–22.

117: C. S. Lewis, *Letters to Malcolm, Chiefly on Prayer*. New York: Harvest, 1963. See pages 27 and 90.

117: "Zeal for your house": John 2:17, quoting Psalm 69:9, various versions of the Bible.

118: "I prayed to my God": Paraphrase of Nehemiah 4–5.

120: "The heavens declare": Psalm 19:1, many versions of Scripture.

121: "The manuscripts of God": Quoted in Ken Gire, *Windows of the Soul*. Grand Rapids: Zondervan, 1996, 205.

123: Receive from God a name: Revelation 19:12.

123: Lewis, *The Problem of Pain*, 154–55.

123: "In my Father's house": John 14:2 NIV.

CHAPTER 8: "AS YOU WISH"

125: C. S. Lewis, "A Slip of the Tongue," in *The Weight of Glory*. New York: Macmillan, 1980, 131.

125: *The Princess Bride*, 1987, directed by Rob Reiner, screenplay by William Goldman, based on the novel *The Princess Bride: S. Morgenstern's Classic Tale of True Love and High Adventure* by William Goldman, published in 1972.

126: "Vanity of vanities": Ecclesiastes 1:2 KJV.

126: "Meaningless, a chasing": Ecclesiastes 2:11, 17, 26; 4:4, 16; 6:9 NIV.

126: Gary W. Moon, *Falling for God: Saying Yes to His Extravagant Proposal.* Colorado Springs: WaterBrook Press, 2004, 75.

127: Jean Pierre de Caussade, *The Sacrament of the Present Moment.* Translated by Kitty Muggeridge. San Francisco: Harper & Row, 1982: Quoted in Richard J. Foster and James Bryan Smith, eds., *Devotional Classics.* San Francisco: HarperSanFrancisco, 1993, 232.

127: "As the Father has loved": John 15:9–10 NRSV.

127: Brother Lawrence, *The Practice of the Presence of God.* Springdale, PA: Whitaker House, 1982, 45.

127: "At the heart of communion": Moon, *Falling for God,* 96.

128: C. S. Lewis, *The Great Divorce.* New York: Macmillan, 1942. Paraphrase from chapter 9.

128: Anne Lamott, *Bird by Bird.* New York: Doubleday/Anchor, 1994, 121.

129: "Whoever believes in me": John 7:38 TNIV.

129: Pharaoh and Moses: See, for example, Exodus 3; 5.

129: King Saul: See 1 Samuel 10:23; 13.

129: David: See, for example, 2 Samuel 5–6; 11–12.

130: Haman and Esther: See Esther 3; 5.

130: Herod: See Matthew 2.

130: "I must decrease": John 3:30, various versions of the Bible.

130: Frank Laubach, *Man of Prayer.* Syracuse, NY: Laubach Literacy International, 1990, 247.

130: Rahab: Joshua 2; 6.

130: Jacob: Genesis 27.

130: Zacchaeus: Luke 19:1–9.

130: "The place where they": Acts 4:31 TNIV.

131: Fruit of the Spirit: Galatians 5:22–23.

131: "The wind blows where": John 3:8.

132: George MacDonald, *Thomas Wingfold, Curate,* chap. 15, "The Lawn." Project Gutenberg EBook #25 at http://us12.us.archive.org/0/texts/8twcc/8twcc10.txt.

133: "Deep calls to deep": Psalm 42:7 NIV.

134: Georgia O'Keeffe: Quoted in Julia Cameron, *The Artist's Way: A Spiritual Path to Higher Creativity.* New York: Putnam, 1992, 22.

134: Anne Dillard, in an essay first appearing in *Life* magazine and later included in *The Meaning of Life*, ed. David Friend and the editors of *Life*. Boston: Little Brown, 1991.

134: John Steinbeck, *East of Eden*. New York: Penguin Books, 2003.

135: "When the grinders": Ecclesiastes 12:3–5 NIV.

135: An old Quaker sect: Quoted in Suzanne Farnham et al., *Listening Hearts: Discerning Call in Community*. Harrisburg, PA: Morehouse Publishing, 1991, 24.

135: If you are thirsty: John 7:37; Revelation 22:17.

136: Lewis, *The Weight of Glory*, 3.

CHAPTER 9: WHEN GOD SEEMS ABSENT

139: St. John of the Cross: "Song of the Soul that delights in knowing God by faith," from *St. John of the Cross: Alchemist of the Soul: His Life, His Poetry, His Prose*. Edited by Antonia T. De Nicholas. York Beach, ME: Samuel Weiser, 1989, 131.

140: Martin E. Marty, *A Cry of Absence: Reflections for the Winter of the Heart*. San Francisco: Harper & Row, 1983.

141: "I cry to you for help": Psalm 88:13–14 NIV.

141: C. S. Lewis, *A Grief Observed*. New York: Bantam Books, 1976, 4.

141: "In the land of Uz": Job 1:1 NIV. Subsequent quotations of Scripture in this section, apart from paraphrases, are from Job 1–3 NIV.

142: Philip Yancey, *The Bible Jesus Read*. Grand Rapids: Zondervan, 1999, 49–50.

144: "Mourn with those": Romans 12:15 TNIV.

145: Yancey, *The Bible Jesus Read*, chapter 2.

146: *Where Is God When*: A play on Philip Yancey, *Where Is God When It Hurts?* Grand Rapids: Zondervan, 1977.

146: He will wipe every tear: See Revelation 7:17; 21:4.

148: "You gave us up": Psalm 44:11–12, 17 NIV.

148: Ellen Davis, *Getting Involved with God: Rediscovering the Old Testament*. Boston: Cowley Publications, 2001, chap. 10.

148: "You crushed us": Psalms 44:19, 23–24; 6:3 NIV.

149: Lewis Smedes, *My God and I*. Grand Rapids: Eerdmans, 2003, 133.

149: "If only I knew": Job 23:3–4.

150: "Then the LORD answered": Job 38:1 NIV.

150: Davis, *Getting Involved with God*, chap. 10.

150: "Who cuts a channel": Job 38:25–27 NIV.

150: "A land where no one lives": Job 38:26 NRSV.

151: Ostrich: Job 39:13, 18 NIV.

151: Hippopotamus: See Job 40:15–24, quotations from NIV, NASB, and paraphrase.

151: Wild oxen: Job 39:9–12.

151: Wild donkey: Job 39:5–8.

151: Mountain goats: Job 39:1–4.

151: Leviathan: Job 41:33 NIV.

151: Annie Dillard: From *Pilgrim at Tinker Creek* in *Three by Annie Dillard: The Writing Life, An American Childhood, Pilgrim at Tinker Creek.* New York: HarperCollins, 1990, 135.

151: "And when I begin": Mallory Ortberg, unpublished manuscript.

152: "My ears had heard": Job 42:5 NIV.

152: "Man of sorrows": Isaiah 53:3, various versions of the Bible.

152: "We considered him": Isaiah 53:4 NIV.

152: "My God, my God": Matthew 27:46, various versions of the Bible.

152: Nicholas Wolterstorff, *Lament for a Son.* Grand Rapids: Eerdmans, 1987, 61.

153: Karl Barth: Quoted in a taped lecture by Nicholas Wolterstorff, n.d.

153: "I am angry": Job 42:7 NIV.

153: Names in the Bible: See, for example, Herbert Lockyer, *All the Men of the Bible.* Grand Rapids: Zondervan, 1958; and Herbert Lockyer, *All the Women of the Bible.* Grand Rapids: Zondervan, 1967.

CHAPTER 10: THE HEDGE

155: Suzanne Farnham et al., *Listening Hearts: Discerning Call in Community.* Harrisburg, PA: Morehouse Publishing, 1991, 27.

157: Philip Yancey, *Rumors of Another World.* Grand Rapids: Zondervan, 2003, 45.

159: "The time has come": Mark 1:15 TNIV.

159: *Monty Python and the Holy Grail*, directed by Terry Gilliam and Terry Jones, written by Graham Chapman and John Cleese, 1975.

160: "Anyone who loves me": John 14:23 TNIV.

160: "I tell you the truth": John 1:51 NIV.

161: "Our Father in heaven": Matthew 6:9–10 TNIV.

161: *Star Trek*: A science-fictional series created for television (1966–69) by Gene Roddenberry and the basis for a later television series (*Star Trek: The Next Generation*) and a number of full-length films.

162: Viktor Frankl, *Man's Search for Meaning.* New York: Washington Square Press, 1963, 81.

162: "Made the two one": Ephesians 2:14, 18 TNIV.

165: "Where can I go?": Psalm 139:7 NIV.

166: "I plan to enroll": Richard Felix, *The School of Dying Graces.* Wheaton, IL: Tyndale House, 2004, 24.

167: "Her personal Gethsemane": Ibid., 3.

BESTSELLING AUTHOR

JOHN ORTBERG

FOREWORD BY DR. HENRY CLOUD

SOUL
KEEPING

CARING *for* THE MOST IMPORTANT
PART *of* YOU

Read an excerpt from

CHAPTER 1

THE SOUL NOBODY
KNOWS

One of the most important words in the Bible is *soul*. We throw that word around a lot, but if someone were to ask you to explain exactly what the word *soul* means, what would you say?

- *Why should I pay attention to my soul?*
- *Hasn't science disproven its existence?*
- *Isn't the soul the province of robe-wearing, herbal-tea drinkers?*
- *Isn't "soul-saving" old-fashioned language that ignores concerns for holistic justice?*
- *Won't it mean preoccupation with navel-gazing? Will I have to go to Big Sur or look at some stranger in the eyes? Will I have to journal?*

Belief in the soul is ubiquitous: "Most people, at most times, in most places, at most ages, have believed that human beings have some kind of souls." We know it matters. We suspect it's important. But we're not sure what it means.

It's the word that won't go away, even though it is used less and less.

From birth to our final resting place ("May God rest his soul"), the soul is our earliest companion and our ultimate concern. The word is ethereal, mysterious, and deep. And a little spooky. ("All Souls' Day" comes two days after Halloween and has always sounded to me like disembodied spirits floating around at the Haunted Mansion in Disneyland.)

How many of our children learned this prayer? How many times have *you* recited it at bedtime?

Now I lay me down to sleep,
I pray the Lord my soul to keep.
If I should die before I wake,
I pray the Lord my soul to take.

What does it mean to ask God "my soul to keep"? If I expire before sunrise, and he takes my soul, what exactly is it that gets taken?

HOW MUCH DOES A SOUL WEIGH?

Jeffrey Boyd is a kind of Don Quixote of the soul. He is a Yale psychiatrist, an ordained minister, and coauthor of *Diagnostic and Statistical Manual of Mental Disorders*, a work in which you will search in vain for a single reference to "soul." It does include something called "depersonalization disorder," a feeling of estrangement from oneself. But Boyd also writes books and articles trying to reinject the word *soul* into our scientific vocabulary.

In one study of hundreds of church attenders, Boyd found that most people believe they know what *soul* means, but when asked to explain it, they can't do it. The soul turns out to be like Supreme Court Justice Potter Stewart's description of obscenity: "It may be hard to define, but I know it when I see it." About half of church attenders adopt what Boyd calls the Looney Tunes Theory of the soul:

If Daffy Duck were blown up with dynamite, then there would
be a transparent image of Daffy Duck that would float up from
the dead body. The translucent image would have wings and
carry a harp. From the air this apparition would speak down
to Bugs Bunny, who set off the dynamite.

It sounds funny to talk about cartoons when it comes to the soul, but as Aristotle said, "The soul never thinks without a picture."

The soul can't be put under a microscope or studied by X-ray. About a hundred years ago a doctor measured the slight weight loss experienced by seven tuberculosis victims at the moment of death, which led him to claim that the soul weighs twenty-one grams. His idea years later created a title for a movie with Sean Penn and Naomi Watts, but it was never duplicated and was widely ridiculed in the medical community. Some are convinced that soul language needs to go.

A philosopher named Owen Flanagan says there is no place in science for the notion of a soul: "Desouling is the primary operation of the scientific image."

But Boyd argues that we see people who have a strength of soul that simply will not be degraded by the humiliation their body puts them through.... The soul knows a glory that the body cannot rob. In some ways, in some cases, the more the body revolts, the more the soul shines through.

THE HIGH AND THE LOW OF THE SOUL

We can't seem to talk about beauty or art without talking about the soul — particularly music. Aretha Franklin is the Queen of Soul. It is possible that if your soul isn't moved by Ray Charles, Otis Redding, Little Richard, Fats Domino, or James Brown, you may want to check to make sure you still have one. Kid Rock wrote "Rebel Soul." A sixteen-year-old, wanna-be pop singer named Jewel hitchhiked to Mexico and watched desperate people looking for help and wrote what would become her breakthrough song: "Who Will Save Your Soul?"

We need the word when we speak of not just the highest, but also the lowest parts of human existence. Over one hundred years ago, W.E.B. Du Bois called his book about the oppressed humanity of a race *The Souls of Black Folk*. No other word would do: *The Selves of Black Folk* does not carry the same dignity. "Soul food" would be the name given for southern cooking that began with slaves who had to survive on whatever leftovers they were given. "Soul power" became the name for a sense of dignity and worth in a people who had been forced to live with none. "Soul brother" reflects the bond that knits together those persecuted because of skin color.

Does soul require suffering to make itself known?

We speak of larger entities having soul. During every election, politicians and pundits warn us that the soul of America is at stake. ServiceMaster CEO William Pollard wrote a leadership book called *The Soul of the Firm*. Shortstop and team captain Derek Jeter has been given the title "soul of the Yankees." Quarterback Tom Brady deemed receiver Wes Walker the "soul" of the New England Patriots. These may be metaphors, but they point to the notion of the soul as that which holds a larger entity together.

SOUL FOR SALE

We speak of the soul as a source of strength, and yet we speak of it as fragile. Something about the soul always seems to be at risk. A soul is something that can be lost or sold. The selling of a soul has been made into countless operas, books, and country music lyrics, as well as a movie called *Bedazzled* and a musical called *Damn Yankees*.... In the television series *The Simpsons*, Homer sells his soul for a donut and then impulsively eats all but one bite, which he puts in the refrigerator with the instructions: "Soul Donut. Do Not Eat." ...

Does a fetus have a soul? A whole debate about abortion rages around this one. Does life happen at conception? Is that when a being becomes human? Plato believed that souls were reincarnated based on how elevated they had been last time around: wise souls come back as seekers of beauty or kings or athletic trainers, whereas cowards come back as women and boozers may come back as donkeys. Augustine said that maybe souls preexist somewhere and then slip into bodies on their own, like people picking out a good car.

We are not sure what the soul is, but the word sells. Advertisers speak of cars being soulful; Kia actually manufactures a car called the Kia Soul. Is it for people who want to go beyond transportation to transmigration? You can also find the Soul Diva (for the "style conscious woman who regards her car as important as her entire outfit"); the Soul Burner (the "bad boy" of the Soul concept); and the Soul Searcher (for the driver focused on "achieving personal inner peace and creating a calm cocoon for occupants").

The word *soul* won't go away, because it speaks somehow of eternity:

> Now there are some things we all know, but we don't take'em out and look at'm very often. We all know that *something* is eternal. And it ain't houses and it ain't names and it ain't earth, and it ain't even the stars.... everybody knows in their bones that *something* is eternal, and that something has to do with human beings. All the greatest people ever lived have been telling us that for five thousand years and yet you'd be surprised how people are always losing hold of it....

A WINDOW TO YOUR SOUL

We speak of the eyes being the window to the soul. Scientists say the eyes can reveal our inner thoughts. For instance, when people are doing hard mental work, their pupils dilate. Daniel Kahneman wrote about researchers monitoring the eyes of subjects trying to solve difficult math problems. They would sometimes surprise subjects by asking them, "Why did you give up just now?"

"How did you know?" the unsuspecting students asked.

"We have a window to your soul."

Psychologist Edmund Hess writes how pupils widen when people look at beautiful nature pictures. When I was in grad school, I saw two famous pictures of a lovely woman—identical, except that in one of them, her pupils are dilated, and that picture is always judged much more attractive. Belladonna, an herb-based drug that expands the pupils, is actually sold as a cosmetic. Professional poker players sometimes wear sunglasses simply to keep their pupils from giving their excitement away.

U.S. President George W. Bush said that when he looked into Russian President Vladimir Putin's eyes, he was able to get a sense of his soul....

When we talk of love, we speak of soul. No one searches for the love of their life on a site called BodyMate.com. In his dialogue *The Symposium*, Plato has Aristophanes present the story of soul mates. Aristophanes states that humans originally had four arms, four legs, and a single head made of two faces, but Zeus feared their power and split them all in half, condemning them to spend their lives searching for the other half to complete them. In the film *Jerry Maguire*, Tom Cruise's character expresses the idea unforgettably to Renée Zellweger: "You complete me." Can one person really complete another? Do we all have one and only one soul mate out there in the world someplace?

Churches are supposed to know about souls. We often sing a song that originated as a psalm: "Bless the Lord, O My Soul." How can your soul bless, or make happy, the Lord? Sometimes we speak of souls as if they are spiritual scalps: certain people who are highly regarded as "soul-winners" or who are especially adept at going after "lost souls." We get teary-eyed at the evangelist who desires to win "just one more soul for Jesus." Old-time evangelist Billy Sunday used to calculate how much money it cost him to save a soul: in Boston in 1911 it was $450. Churches did the job more economically: Congregationalists came in at $70 per soul, Baptists at $70, and Methodists at a staggeringly low $3.12—which was cheap even by the 1911 standards!

The universal distress signal, SOS, is said to stand for "Save Our Souls." What does it mean for a soul to be saved?

"I don't deserve a soul, yet I still have one," writes Douglas Coupland. "I know because it hurts." ...

We search for the soul because we're curious. But not just that. The search for the soul always begins with our great hurt.

If I should die before I wake, I pray the Lord my soul to take ...

What is the soul?

SOURCES

"Most people, at most times": Mark Baker and Stewart Goetz, *The Soul Hypothesis* (New York: Continuum Books, 2011), 100.

"If Daffy Duck were": Jeffrey Boyd, *Soul Psychology* (Colorado Springs: Soul Research Institute, 1994), 59.

Soul weighs twenty-one grams: Les Parrott, *You're Stronger Than You Think* (Carol Stream, IL: Tyndale, 2012), 116.

Owen Flanagan: Baker and Goetz, *The Soul Hypothesis*, 100.

William Pollard, *The Soul of the Firm* (Grand Rapids: Zondervan, 2000).

W.E.B Du Bois, *The Souls of Black Folk* (Healdburg, CA: Eucalyptus Press, 2013).

Plato believed that souls were re-incarnated: Steward Goetz and Charles Taliaferro, *A Brief History of the Soul* (Malden, MA: Wiley-Blackwell, 2011), 12.

Augustine said that maybe souls preexist: Ibid., 44–45.

"Now there are some things": Thornton Wilder, *Our Town* (New York: Harper & Row, 1938), 87–88.

Edmund Hess: cited in Daniel Kahneman, *Thinking Fast and Slow* (New York: Farrar, Straus, and Giroux, 2011), 32.

"soulful work" movement: www.soulfulwork.net

cost to save soul: The New York Times (October 9, 1911), section 7.

"I don't deserve a soul": Douglas Coupland, *The Gum Thief* (New York: Bloomsbury, 2007), 21.

"If a child is born": Jeffrey Boyd, "One's Self-Concept and Biblical Theology," *Journal of the Evangelical Theological Society* 40:2 (June 1997): 223.

Willow Creek Association
Vision, Training, Resources for Prevailing Churches

This resource was created to serve you and to help you build a local church that prevails. It is just one of many ministry tools that are part of the Willow Creek Resources® line, published by the Willow Creek Association together with Zondervan.

The Willow Creek Association (WCA) was created in 1992 to serve a rapidly growing number of churches from across the denominational spectrum that are committed to helping unchurched people become fully devoted followers of Christ. Membership in the WCA now numbers over 10,500 Member Churches worldwide from more than ninety denominations.

The Willow Creek Association links like-minded Christian leaders with each other and with strategic vision, training, and resources in order to help them build prevailing churches designed to reach their redemptive potential. Here are some of the ways the WCA does that.

- **A2: Building Prevailing Acts 2 Churches—Today**—an annual two-and-a-half day event, held at Willow Creek Community Church in South Barrington, Illinois, to explore strategies for building churches that reach out to seekers and build believers, and to discover new innovations and breakthroughs from Acts 2 churches around the country.

- **The Leadership Summit**—a once a year, two-and-a-half-day conference to envision and equip Christians with leadership gifts and responsibilities. Presented live at Willow Creek as well as via satellite broadcast to over one hundred locations across North America, this event is designed to increase the leadership effectiveness of pastors, ministry staff, volunteer church leaders, and Christians in the marketplace.

- **Ministry-Specific Conferences**—throughout each year the WCA hosts a variety of conferences and training events—both at Willow Creek's main campus and offsite, across the U.S., and around the world—targeting church leaders and volunteers in ministry-specific areas such as: evangelism, small groups, preaching and teaching, the arts, children, students, women, volunteers, stewardship, raising up resources, etc.

- **Willow Creek Resources®**—provides churches with trusted and field-tested ministry resources in such areas as leadership, evangelism, spiritual formation, spiritual gifts, small groups, stewardship, student ministry, children's ministry, the use of the arts-drama, media, contemporary music—and more.

- **WCA Member Benefits**—includes substantial discounts to WCA training events, a 20 percent discount on all Willow Creek Resources®, *Defining Moments* monthly audio journal for leaders, quarterly *Willow* magazine, access to a Members-Only section on WillowNet, monthly communications, and more. Member Churches also receive special discounts and premier services through WCA's growing number of ministry partners—Select Service Providers—and save an average of $500 annually depending on the level of engagement.

For specific information about WCA conferences, resources, membership, and other ministry services contact:

Willow Creek Association
P.O. Box 3188, Barrington, IL 60011-3188
Phone: 847-570-9812, Fax: 847-765-5046
www.willowcreek.com